LYNN A. ROBINSON

trust your gut

HOW THE
POWER
OF
INTUITION
CAN GROW
YOUR BUSINESS

KAPLAN PUBLISHING

This publication is designed to provide accurate and authoritative information in regard to the subject matter covered. It is sold with the understanding that the publisher is not engaged in rendering legal, accounting, or other professional service. If legal advice or other expert assistance is required, the services of a competent professional should be sought.

Note: Real names, as well as pseudonyms, are used throughout the book.

President, Kaplan Publishing: Roy Lipner
Vice President and Publisher: Maureen McMahon
Acquisitions Editor: Michael Cunningham
Development Editor: Trey Thoelcke
Production Editor: Karen Goodfriend
Typesetter: Ellen Gurak
Cover Designer: Jody Billert, Design Literate

Published by Kaplan Publishing,
a division of Kaplan, Inc.

Printed in the United States of America

06 07 08   10 9 8 7 6 5 4 3 2

Library of Congress Cataloging-in-Publication Data

Robinson, Lynn A.
 Trust your gut : how the power of intuiting can grow your business / Lynn A. Robinson.
   p. cm.
 Includes index.
 ISBN-13: 978-1-4195-8440-4
 ISBN-10: 1-4195-8440-5
 1. Success in business–Psychological aspects. 2. Intuition. 3. Decision making–Psychological aspects. 4. Self-actualization (Psychology) 5. Businesspeople–Psychology. I. Title.
 HF5386.R535 2006
 658.4'03–dc22   2006016493

Kaplan Publishing books are available at special quantity discounts to use for sales promotions, employee premiums, or educational purposes. Please call our Special Sales Department to order or for more information at 800-621-9621, ext. 4444, e-mail kaplanpubsales@kaplan.com, or write to Kaplan Publishing, 30 South Wacker Drive, Suite 2500, Chicago, IL 60606-7481.

To my husband, Gary.
I'm glad I trusted my gut.

CONTENTS

INTRODUCTION

Business is about making money. But it's also about making decisions. There are relatively small decisions—when to call a meeting; which e-mail to answer; whether to answer the phone. Then there are big ones, the ones that can make or break your business—which product to launch; who to hire for the CFO position; when we should go public.

How do you make good decisions, not just some of the time, but *all* of the time? Would you say the answer lies in doing the research, getting the facts, and taking time to analyze the details? You'd be right. But what do you do when logic and analysis don't give you what you need? Or the data you've analyzed is filled with conflicting information and you can't make sense of it?

The answer is . . . intuition. Also known as gut feeling, instinct, sixth sense, inner knowing. Malcolm Gladwell writes in his best-selling book *Blink: The Power of Thinking Without Thinking,* "I believe that the task of making sense of ourselves and our behavior requires that we acknowledge there can be as much value in the blink of an eye as in months of rational analysis."

In their classic book *Megatrends,* John Naisbitt and Patricia Aburdene inform us, "Intuition becomes increasingly valuable in the new information society precisely because there is so much data." Even Microsoft founder Bill Gates readily admits that he often relies on intuition.

It sounds so easy when you're faced with a challenging decision and someone suggests that you simply "trust your gut." Or when a colleague with an enviable record of successful stock trades tells you, "I just go with my instincts." But how easy is it?

Some people have called intuition a "quiet inner voice." Those of you who are intrigued by its potential usefulness, yet haven't learned to listen to it, may simply wish you could figure out a way to turn up the volume!

Is intuition better than cold, hard facts? That depends! There are decisions that require logic and analysis. You may have the rational information necessary to easily make the right decision. But there are times when you have nothing to go on, no information on which to base your determination. That's when knowing how to access your intuition can be most helpful.

However you do it, consciously using intuition is becoming more prevalent. Indeed, a survey that was conducted in May 2002 by executive search firm Christian & Timbers reveals that fully 45 percent of corporate executives now rely more on instinct than on facts and figures in running their businesses.

According to a recent survey in *BusinessWeek* magazine, "intuition" has become one of the top buzzwords in business. I'm not surprised. It's been simmering on the back burner of the culture stove for years, but now it's beginning to bubble, and I fully expect (dare I say "predict") that it will be at a full roiling boil in a very short time.

I've written five books so far, each of them dealing in different ways with the increasingly popular topic of intuition. I've been teaching people about intuition for over two decades. At the start of my business, my client base consisted largely of folks interested in New Age spirituality. Today my work is more likely to include entrepreneurs and CEOs interested in tapping the inner resources of their intuition to help them find answers to life and business challenges.

There have been other changes. What used to be an almost exclusively female clientele has become an almost even split between men and women. I got a hint of this impending shift when, about ten years ago, my then 12-year-old stepson attended one of my classes and actually took more notes than any of the 30 or so women in attendance.

So why so much more interest in intuition today? I doubt that anyone knows for sure, but my guess is that the tidal wave of information that's flooded the shores of our minds has overwhelmed our ability to categorize and analyze.

We simply can't seem to generate satisfactory conclusions or make good decisions anymore, and so we turn—consciously or unconsciously—to that amazing sense we were born with. We turn to our intuition—our "inner knowing," our "sixth sense," our "gut instinct"—and we find to our surprise and great relief that the answer has been there all along.

So what is this "magical" decision-making tool that so many titans of industry credit for their success? Is it available to only a gifted few? Or is it a skill mere mortals can develop? You'll find the answers in these pages, filled with ideas, tools, and exercises designed to help you learn to trust your gut and grow your business.

CHAPTER 1

TRUST YOUR WHAT?

Your intuition is your direct pipeline to a form of intelligence that is completely beyond your conscious brain. Successful, effective, happy people are those who have gotten onto the beam of their own intuitive senses and who rely continuously on their inner guidance – and they seldom make mistakes.

— BRIAN TRACY, BEST-SELLING AUTHOR, CONSULTANT, AND SPEAKER

You've seen it mentioned in just about every business book in the past decade. It's the declaration that it's important to "Trust your gut." It sounds so easy when you read it or when someone exhorts you to "Go with your instincts," "Listen to your inner voice," "Heed your intuition." It almost sounds as if there's a magic switch labeled "INSIGHT NOW" that others are able to turn on at a moment's notice and instantly receive wise counsel.

Were you asleep in business class when the professor went over instructions about listening to your intuition? Were you out the day he spoke about the importance of intuition as a decision-making tool? Did you get the correct answer on the quiz when asked the percentage of senior executives who attribute intuition to their success? (Hint: The answer is 90 percent.) The sad news is, in all likelihood, intuition wasn't mentioned at all.

Thought Leaders on Intuition

Yet listen to these thought leaders and philosophers and businesspeople and scientists who proclaim the importance of this inner wisdom.

Jonas Salk, the developer of the polio vaccine, writes, "The intuitive mind tells the logical mind where to look next."

Warren Bennis, a best-selling author of 20 books on leadership, change, and management, calls intuition his "inner voice" and says that listening to it and trusting it is one of the most important leadership lessons he has learned.

W. Brian Arthur is a professor of operations research at the Santa Fe Institute. He teaches a highly scientific, mathematical way of strategizing and of making decisions. Even he is a believer in intuition, stating, "For the big decisions in life, you need to reach a deeper region of consciousness. Making a decision, then, becomes not so much about 'deciding' as about letting an inner wisdom emerge."

Clothing designer Donna Karan posits that "One of our greatest gifts is our intuition. It is a sixth sense we all have—we just need to learn to tap into and trust it."

Howard Gardner, professor of cognition and education at Harvard University, believes an intuitive leap can mark a breakthrough. "When you're entering an area where the unknowns are high and experience is important, if you don't rely on intuition you're cutting yourself short."

Richard Branson, the entrepreneurial founder of Virgin Airlines and Virgin Records, states, "I rely far more on gut instinct than researching huge amounts of statistics."

Buckminster Fuller, the futurist, architect, and inventor with 28 patents to his name, was a big believer in using the power of inner wisdom to create an extraordinary life. "Intuition often turns dreams into demonstrable fact."

What Is Intuition?

Intuition is a resource that, if nurtured, can lead to increased sales, profitable investments, creative inventions, successful hires, advantageous negotiations, bigger profits, and increased accuracy in forecasting business trends.

Intuition is a skill we all have. Survey after survey indicates that decision makers in a wide variety of fields rely on it to make successful decisions and choices. We're born with intuition. Perhaps some of us have the ability to tap into it more easily than do others. But like any skill, the more we practice using it, the better we get at it.

What is this gift of intuition? How do we define it? Here are some ways it's commonly described.

- A tool for quick and ready insight
- A natural mental faculty
- A gut feeling
- A sixth sense
- An inner knowing
- An instinct
- A hunch
- Wisdom from a Higher Power
- A still, quiet inner voice

Where does it come from? There are two schools of thought about the origins of intuition.

1. Synthesis of prior knowledge—A blend of logic, experience, and subconscious information that's stored in your mind and recalled when needed

2. A Higher Power—Divine intelligence, a "compass of the soul" that guides, informs, and directs you toward success.

Synthesis of Prior Knowledge

To folks in the first category, intuition is a matter of recognizing patterns or cues that ultimately show you what to do. An intuitive firefighter will tell you he saw a pattern to the blaze that made him issue a command to evacuate the building immediately. Later, if pressed on his decision, he might be able to state that the flames were acting in a strange manner, and that fact, combined with a certain smell and roar from the building, indicated an imminent explosion.

He had correctly ascertained that if he didn't get the occupants and his team out of the structure, he would lose lives. With seconds to make a decision, he processed complex information based on years of knowledge to make what appeared to others around him to be an instinctual act.

An executive interviewing for a key position dismisses one of the applicants, who later turns out to have lied on her résumé. When asked how he knew something was wrong, he simply alluded to a gut feeling. However, when questioned more deeply on what raised a red flag about the applicant, he was able to expand on his response. He noted the fact that the interviewee didn't maintain eye contact when answering several key questions. She had shifted uncomfortably in her chair when asked about her responsibilities in a prior position. He also noticed that her response was a bit overenthusiastic to a subtler question.

A Higher Power

While both the firefighter and executive noted above might point to intuition as a form of pattern recognition, many people also view intuition as a form of spiritual inner guidance. Mark Fisher writes in his book *The Instant Millionaire:*

> *Listen to that tiny inner voice sleeping in the depths of your mind and give it more freedom to express itself. The more often you repeat the formula, the more powerful it will become and the more surely it will guide you. This is your intuition, the voice of your soul–the road to your secret power.*

Sarah Ban Breathnach, president and CEO of Simple Abundance, Inc., and best-selling author of the *Simple Abundance* series of books, defines intuition as "the subliminal sense that spirit endowed us with to maneuver safely through the maze of real life."

Katy Wells describes receiving this "message from her spirit" version of intuition prior to opening her interior decorating business:

> *I had prayed to be guided to the right career after my husband died. The inner voice I associate with my intuition kept nudging me towards 'hanging out my shingle.' I also had recurring dreams about decorating people's homes. Finally, after a series of synchronicities that continued to point me in this direction, I found an ideal storefront to rent as my office and landed two clients, all within the same week. This was seven years ago and I've had a bustling and thriving business ever since.*

Practice

So what is intuition? Is it immediate knowledge based on past experience and pattern recognition? Or is it guidance that comes to us from a spiritual source? The consensus is that despite these differences, both explanations are valid. We're going to explore both types of intuition because whichever one you believe, you're right!

We all receive intuitive information. Like any skill, the more you practice it, the more you'll improve. As you continue to develop this talent, you'll find you rely on it more and more. The process will no longer feel laborious. It will simply be a matter of checking in with it. "What's my gut say?" and the answer appears. You'll recognize those inner nudges pointing you in the direction of success and away from bad decisions.

Practice opens up the information flow of intuitive insights. You'll find that answers come unbidden, popping into your mind, offering up creative solutions, steering you toward prosperity, toward strong leadership and profitable connections with others, and, overall, toward a happier outlook. And there's a big bonus: You won't be bogged down in hours of analysis and research anymore.

It really does work like that—which is why one of the best decisions you could make right now is to begin to develop your intuition.

As one of my banking executive clients said recently, "I use my intuition to come up with the right answer and then use my logic and research skills to prove what I already knew."

Think back on the past week. Describe an occasion when you had a hunch about something. How did you receive the information? Did it come as a flash of insight? A gut feeling? An inner knowing? Perhaps you had a dream or heard an inner voice.

Did you follow this hunch or cast it aside?

Did your intuition prove to be accurate?

As you begin to pay attention to the many ways you receive intuition, you'll be rewarded with an *increasing* flow of accurate and reliable insight.

The Gut Trusters Quiz

Perhaps you're already a "Gut Truster" and don't even realize you have this skill or talent. Take this brief quiz to find out.

Yes No

☐   ☐   I frequently get a flash of insight that leads to a creative idea or insight.

☐   ☐   I often act on hunches that turn out to be right.

☐   ☐   I tune in to how I'm feeling before I make a decision.

☐   ☐   I've argued against an "obvious" or "logical" decision because I just "knew" it wasn't right.

☐   ☐   I do a "gut check" before moving in a new direction.

☐   ☐   I act on the intuitive information I receive.

☐   ☐   I pay attention to my first impression of a new person or situation.

☐   ☐   My intuitive insights help me solve problems at work as well as in my personal life.

☐   ☐   My friends and colleagues often call on me to mediate a disagreement because I'm able to "see all sides."

☐   ☐   I've had a dream that helped me resolve a problem or come up with a creative solution.

☐   ☐   Intuition enables me to have insight into others' behavior that allows me to resolve difficulties more quickly.

Scoring

- Eleven yes answers: Congratulations! You have a very high "IQ" (Intuition Quotient.) Increase your conscious use of it and it will serve you even better.
- Six to 10 yes answers: Begin to pay attention to all the ways you receive intuitive impressions and you'll raise your "IQ" in no time.
- Three or fewer yes answers: Time to get out of your head! There is more to life than logic and rationality. Be willing to experiment with using intuition in low-risk situations. You'll build your "intuition muscles" and be rewarded with quick and ready insight in no time.

Throughout this book, I'll give you tools, information, and intuitive success stories from fellow businesspeople. In fact, I predict that with practice your intuition will have become an old friend by the time you finish the last chapter—a friend who can be counted on for good advice and guidance.

gut truster tip

Intuition is a resource that, if nurtured, can lead to increased sales, profitable investments, creative inventions, successful hires, advantageous negotiations, bigger profits, and increased accuracy in forecasting business trends.

CHAPTER 2

Listen to Your Intuition

Organizational effectiveness does not lie in that narrow-minded concept called rationality. It lies in the blend of clearheaded logic and powerful intuition.

— HENRY MINTZBERG, AUTHOR OF *MANAGERS NOT MBAS*

Steve Lishansky, cofounder and senior partner of Koanetic Consulting, describes how intuition helped him land his first major corporate client. His friend Bob had put him in touch with Tony, an information technology officer at a financial services company. Steve told me he had felt a bit daunted as he had never dealt with information technology *or* financial services, but he knew that if he were going to grow his business, he needed to make the call.

"So Steve," Tony said after a quick handshake and a brief introduction, "Bob says you'd be worth talking to about our project. What do you do?" Steve didn't hesitate. He jumped right in with an intuitive flash that set up the whole conversation. He told me the information he needed to help him win this account simply popped into his head. "I help companies improve their performance," he said to Tony. "Rather than bore you with a laundry list of what we do, why don't you give me a few of your specific issues, and I'll be specific about what I'd do with them." Tony raised an eyebrow, then proceeded to list his organizational challenges. As they started to converse, Steve began to see questions appear in his mind. He was surprised but not *too* surprised. He was, after all, an intuition "believer," so he simply relaxed, followed his intuition, and asked Tony the questions that presented themselves.

As Tony answered the questions, he became excited. "I never thought of it that way before," he exclaimed. Steve asked more questions and Tony answered them all, and at the end of the meeting he told Steve they had worked with another consultant for four frustrating months trying to get him to understand what they were after. "And in just one hour," Tony said, "you not only got it, but I'm really clear about how you can help us!"

Bottom line: Tony introduced Steve to his boss—the CIO—who was similarly impressed, and Steve, with the help of his intuition, had his first Fortune 500 assignment. Over the course of the relationship, it turned out to be worth over a million dollars. Steve says of that day, "You know, it was an absolutely effortless conversation. An insightful line of questioning just kept on appearing, and as Tony answered the questions, he was led to greater and greater clarity. At the end of the conversation Tony made an amazing statement. He said, 'You know, if my people could do with their clients what you just did with me, we'd have no problems.' I knew at that moment what an extraordinary meeting had just taken place. As it turned out, we produced dramatic, highly valued results for their organization. Tony became a friend, and this company became my best client for the next seven years."

What You'll Hear

Steve listened to his intuition at a critical moment in his business life. He heard it. He heeded it. And he scored a major contract. But listening to your intuition doesn't always lead directly to the bottom line. Nevertheless, there are plenty of times when it's important to tune in and listen up. For example:

- When there's insufficient data
- When you need to make a decision quickly
- When there's too much information
- When the data is conflicting
- When your data seems to support several different options
- When your individual or group vision has become cloudy
- When you're stuck and can't "think" your way out
- When you need to come up with outside-the-box ideas

There is no right or wrong way to receive intuitive information. However, you probably have a predominant mode of receiving its wisdom. Here are some common ways intuition communicates.

Physical Sensations

You may experience this as a knot in your stomach, hot flash, cold shivers, a tension in your neck or shoulders, or a generalized sense of lightness or heaviness.

My client Edward described a decision he had to make in the spring of 2005. His company had decided to expand its operations and open branch offices in four key cities in the United States. There had been a good deal of money and time invested in research and analysis as to which geographical area would be most profitable for the company. Whenever he met with his staff to work on logistical details about the sites for the business expansion, he had what he describes as a "knot in my stomach" about one of the cities. The other three locations that were chosen he felt great about. The city that caused his indigestion? New Orleans—the area devastated by Hurricane Katrina in October 2005.

Emotion

Intuitive information often comes through your emotions. Feelings of relief, enthusiasm, passion, eagerness, and excitement characterize good decisions. Conversely, if you're making a decision that may lead you astray, you'll likely feel heavy, depressed, weighted down, drained, bored, or enervated.

You've been feeling overwhelmed lately and realize you need to examine your lifestyle with an eye to letting go of some activities. As you examine your list of items, which of them do you look at and immediately feel drained? Which things make you feel excited? Those responses are your intuition at work! Move away or let go of the ones that deplete you and keep the ones that energize you.

Auditory

Many people report a "still, quiet inner voice." It may sound perceptively different from your normal everyday inner chatter. People often characterize it as a nonjudgmental or compassionate voice.

My fledgling intuitive consulting business began 20 years ago as the result of this type of intuition. I walked into a funeral service for a friend who had just passed away. I heard an inner voice saying "Sit there." My attention was drawn to an empty seat next to one of the few people in the room I didn't know. Always a believer in trusting these auditory messages, I sat next to her. The short version of the story is that my seatmate turned out to be a reporter for the *Boston Globe* newspaper. She wrote a story about my unusual consulting business. As a result, over 300 people called me to request my services and my new career was born.

Image

The old adage "A picture is worth a thousand words" pertains to this form of intuitive information. Intuition often communicates through symbolic images.

My client Karen was seeking venture capital money for her skin care product line. She had presented her business plan at an investors' meeting and had the happy outcome of two groups seemingly interested in working with her. They presented equally attractive offers. As she studied her pros and cons list, she felt more and more confused about which one to work with.

I asked her to close her eyes, take a deep breath, relax, and envision each of the two offers with the intention of receiving an intuitive response. Within a few moments she opened her eyes and laughed. She had seen an image of one of the potential investors holding a huge sign that said, "My way!" The insight she received was that this individual was probably rather difficult to work with, only wanting to do things *his* way. Karen perceived through this image that he was not particularly collaborative, an issue that was of utmost importance to her. She later had her symbolic instinct confirmed when talking with another person who had worked with this investor.

Epiphany

Otherwise known as "aha" moments, epiphanies are usually flashes of insight or "knowing." People often report they suddenly know something but don't know where the insight came from. Epiphanies often arrive when you least expect them—while showering, washing the dishes, walking the dog, whenever.

Thomas Edison, one of the most prolific inventors of all time, was a great believer in intuition. He registered a new patent on an average of every two weeks during his adult life. He carried a 200-page notebook with him at all times for recording flashes of inspiration. As one biographer described it, Edison would be talking with friends or eating "when something he saw, a topic of conversation, or an intruding memory, jogged up a technological possibility." At the time of his death, Edison had filled 3,400 such notebooks.

Dreams

Dreams can provide a rich source of guidance for insight in all forms when you learn how to use them. The painter Vincent van Gogh once said, "I dream my painting, and then I paint my dream." People report coming up with creative solutions, answers to complex issues, moneymaking ideas, and inventions all while sound asleep.

When I met the *Boston Globe* reporter, I was still working as an operations manager for a software company. Gaining over 300 clients virtually overnight might be some people's idea of a dream come true. To me it was anxiety producing. I was fearful of giving up my "normal" job, with benefits and a weekly paycheck, to be out on my own as a consultant. "Could I keep both jobs?" was the question I asked myself as I drifted off to sleep. When I awakened in the morning, I had to laugh. In my dream, I was out on a lake in *canoes*. Yes, plural! I had one foot in one canoe and the other foot in another canoe, and they were headed in opposite directions! I took that as a very clear sign that I wasn't meant to begin my consulting business while holding on to my day job. I gave my notice that day and never looked back.

If using intuition is new to you, keep reading! You'll find a wealth of information on these pages to get you started. If you're an old hand at intuition and you've been listening to it for years, you, too, can expect to find new techniques, ideas, and processes that will deepen your connection to this wellspring of knowledge.

gut truster tip

Intuitive information primarily communicates through feelings, images, dreams, an inner voice, and physical sensations.

CHAPTER 3

Choose Success

*One decision-making tool–human intuition–seems to offer a reliable
alternative to painstaking fact-gathering and analysis. A survey that was
conducted in May 2002 by executive search firm Christian & Timbers
reveals that fully 45 percent of corporate executives now rely more on
instinct than on facts and figures in running their businesses.*

— HARVARD BUSINESS REVIEW

"Intuition is that unexplainable response to a situation—a knowing. When it's challenged by those around me who rely on data, it will not waver." Jean, the president and CEO of an Alabama-based service company explained further: "If it does waver, then I downgrade the experience from a hunch to simply my ego talking." She laughed and added, "And I'm old enough to know that my ego is my least reliable source!"

Jean described a "feeling" she had after Hurricane Ivan devastated her region in September 2004:

*I felt strongly that we needed to draw against a $1,000,000 line of credit from
the bank. My COO disagreed. He felt the commitment to stewardship and*

budgeting would keep us from needing the 'line.' I didn't want to undermine him so I backed off.

It's now clear that I should have trusted my instincts. After surviving Hurricane Ivan, we were hit with Hurricane Katrina. That line of credit would have made all the difference in surviving the understandable hit we took from the weather-related disasters.

I have struggled and negotiated with the bank and experienced difficulties in both my business and personal life. I have lost the leverage I would have had if I had trusted and acted on my intuition.

We've all made these types of decisions. Some business veterans who have made bad choices and gone against their gut instincts refer to these as the "woulda, coulda, shoulda" experience. If I *would* have trusted my intuition, I *could* have done well, and this better thing *should* have happened.

Good Choice/Bad Choice

To help you determine whether a choice you're making is the best direction to follow, try this. Write several sentences on a notepad about a decision you're about to make. *For the purpose of this exercise, give yourself two options*: Choice A *and* Choice B.

Imagine yourself making the decision to go with Choice A. Close your eyes and ask yourself the following three questions. Then repeat the exercise with Choice B.

1. "How do I feel about this decision?"
   ❑ Up. Enthusiastic
   ❑ Down. Depressed
2. "How do I physically experience this decision?"
   ❑ Lightness, openness, flexibility
   ❑ Tightening of stomach or shoulders at the thought of pursuing this choice

3. "Do I receive any visual impressions when thinking about this choice?"
   - ❑ Positive images surround the symbolic representation of this decision
   - ❑ I see an X through the decision, or I see some other negative image

Of course these are just illustrations of the many ways intuition might speak to you about whether you're about to make a good choice or a bad one. Part of learning to develop your intuition is becoming familiar with the ways in which it communicates to you. You have your own personalized way you receive the information.

In fact, it's much like learning a foreign language. At first it may be unfamiliar to you, yet with practice you begin to notice subtle nuances, shades, and characteristics that allow you to recognize the intuitive messages.

The One-Minute Intuition Checklist

Here's another way to see if you're on the right track with a decision you're about to make. Take the following quick quiz to see how your intuition measures up.

1. Think of a problem or challenge you're facing. Write a few paragraphs about it in your journal or PDA.
2. Now think of *one* possible course of action. Summarize it into a sentence. "My decision is..."
3. Hold that decision in your mind as you go through the following checklist.

Yes No
❑   ❑   Do you feel excited or energized by this decision?
❑   ❑   Do you feel open to making this change?

 ❑   ❑   You know you have other choices, but does this one feel right?

 ❑   ❑   Is this the right time to act on this decision?

 ❑   ❑   Does this decision feel right in your gut?

 ❑   ❑   Can you see the successful completion of this decision?

 ❑   ❑   Close your eyes and think of an image that represents this decision. Did you receive a positive image?

Your One-Minute Intuition Analysis

0 No answers: Your intuition is giving you a clear go-ahead. It's time to take action!

1 No answer: Try to modify your decision and see if it affects your score in a positive direction.

2 No answers: Perhaps your decision required a leap of faith that was a little too big. Are there some smaller steps you could take?

3 No answers: Timing is always important in decision making. If you didn't receive a resounding yes! from your intuition, now may not be the right time for you to make a change.

4 No answers: You're feeling anxious. It's normal to feel at least a little anxious when something changes in our life. Is there part of the decision you could adjust that would make you more comfortable?

5 or more
No answers: Stop! Your intuition is telling you this is clearly not a good decision for you.

Trusting the Choice

The problematic part of using intuition is that often you don't know *why* you're being guided toward or away from something until after the fact. A client, Jake, recently related a story about his plan to buy a second home in California. He knew it was in an area that was experiencing a big real estate boom, and he wanted to buy now while he could still afford the kind of home he and his wife wanted. They worked with a real estate broker and identified the perfect house. It was in a community they liked. It was a short walk to the beach, and some close friends lived nearby.

Everything was perfect except that Jake found he kept putting off the decision to say yes and move ahead on the deal. According to Jake:

> *I'm not usually a procrastinator. I think of myself as a decisive person. Besides that, I had run all the numbers. Everything checked out. It appeared to be a slam-dunk decision.*
>
> *This was becoming a somewhat serious issue between my wife and me. But I couldn't shake the feeling that this wasn't a good decision. I just couldn't figure out why! It was driving me crazy. Fortunately the decision was taken out of my hands when the broker called and told us the sellers were going to accept an offer from another party.*

Several months later Jake was watching the news. The reporter was describing how fires were engulfing the community they'd been interested in. High winds were fanning the flames, and many of the expensive homes were being destroyed. Camera crews captured a scene of firefighters working to douse flames on a familiar-looking place. "Suddenly," Jake said, "I realized this was 'our' house I was looking at, and then it all made sense. I felt awful for the people who owned the place. It could easily have been us. But I also felt thankful I had trusted my gut."

gut truster tip

Intuition is like learning a foreign language. At first it may be unfamiliar to you, yet with practice you begin to notice subtle nuances, shades, and characteristics that allow you to recognize the intuitive messages.

CHAPTER 4

Great Questions Get Great Answers

Successful people engage that creative part of their minds and ask, "Well, I wonder how else I can look at this problem? I wonder how else I could deal with this decision? I wonder what other possibilities I have there?"

— JIM ROHN, BUSINESS PHILOSOPHER, SPEAKER, AND AUTHOR

John describes the morning he was sitting at his desk beleaguered by a sense of failure. He had a headache. His phone hadn't rung all day. He hadn't felt this way earlier in the year when he left the advertising agency he was working for in order to start his own graphic design firm.

If you could have heard the thoughts going through John's mind, you would have discovered he had a very pessimistic focus that morning. Listen in...

- "Why aren't any of these new business initiatives working?"
- "Am I in the wrong business?"
- "Why is Sue having luck with her new business and I'm not?"
- "Have I come into this business at precisely the wrong time?"
- "Why am I having endless problems with my subcontractors?"

- "Will I ever make serious money?"
- "What am I doing wrong?"

Have you ever tried talking with a friend who was stuck in a negative thinking pattern similar to John's? If so, you may have offered one constructive suggestion after another and received little or no response. Your friend was basically not open to your contribution.

Intuition operates in much the same way. If your mind is closed to new ideas, there's simply no room for inspired input from your eager-to-help inner consultant.

Asking the Right Question

When John began to recognize that his unhelpful mental state wasn't producing the answers he needed, he began to shift his focus. He said he remembers something I had said in one of our consulting sessions. "The quality of the questions you ask yourself will determine the quality of the answers you get back." He realized he wasn't asking very good questions!

Edward de Bono, a leading authority on creativity thinking, wrote, "Sometimes the situation is only a problem because it is looked at in a certain way. Looked at in another way, the right course of action may be so obvious that the problem no longer exists."

John realized that all of his concerns were focused on the theme "What am I doing wrong?" His whole internal concentration was on *what's wrong*. In de Bono's way of thinking, he was asking the wrong question. John decided to grab his laptop and sit outside in the early summer sun. Listening to the birds sing put him into a slightly better mood. He began to write about what he wanted to create in his business:

- Clients I enjoy working with who refer me to other great clients
- A monthly net income of at least $10,000

- An easy and enjoyable lifestyle that allows time for me to attend my kids' after-school and weekend events
- A great team of subcontractors I can count on to deliver an excellent product or service
- Positive press for my graphic design business

As John continued his list, he found himself in an even better frame of mind. His thinking was clearer. He felt open to new possibilities. Ideas began to pop into his head.

As he sat outside basking in the sun, he began to shift his focus to questions such as "How can I increase my visibility?" or "What can I do to attract my favorite types of clients?" He discovered that when he was more open-minded and less down on himself and his efforts, the answers that would lead him to success began to come to him more easily.

By the end of his self-imposed break, he had come up with some creative marketing ideas as well as a new approach to provide incentives to current clients who introduced him to new ones. Best of all, when he got back to his office he found that a potential new client had called with an interesting design project.

Sally had a slightly different situation. She'd been out of work for four months and was feeling a little desperate to be back and involved in her career as a CIO in the banking industry. A single mother with a 14-year-old daughter, her last position ended when her former bank was merged with a larger one. She was networking with everyone she knew and had been on several job interviews that sounded promising. But so far, no firm offers.

Sally was a type-A personality in the best of circumstances, and she was finding the lack of structure in her newly jobless life a bit overwhelming. She tried to fill up each day with endless to-do lists and appointments that kept her mind and body occupied.

At the end of one Friday afternoon she collapsed on her sofa in tears. Her ex-husband had picked up their daughter and she faced a weekend by herself. A flood of worries encompassed her. "What if I don't find another CIO job? Maybe I should be thinking of another type of position. What if I don't have what it takes? What if I get an offer in another area of the country? How will that affect my daughter?" The more she thought about her life and career in this way, the more upset she got.

At the end of an hour of frantic worrying, she uncharacteristically fell asleep. She awoke again at around 8:00 and made some dinner. She realized she felt a little calmer. One question seemed to keep forming in her mind: "What can I do to be at peace?"

That was a very different kind of question for Sally to ask herself. Always frantic and on the go at both her former job and at home, she'd never really stopped to consider the idea of being at peace. It was a totally foreign notion. Simply asking the question made her feel calmer and more in harmony with life.

She sat down with her reheated take-out food, left over from last night's dinner, and felt open to a new direction. The fear she had felt washed away, and suddenly the world seemed full of possibilities.

Framing the Questions

Best-selling author Brian Tracy writes, "A major stimulant to creative thinking is focused questions. There is something about a well-worded question that often penetrates to the heart of the matter and triggers new ideas and insights."

What are examples of the focused questions that Tracy refers to? Think about some of the concerns and challenges you face today in your business or at your office. Instead of worrying about them, form them into a question that will evoke intuitive answers. In order to do this most effectively, avoid questions that would suggest a yes or no answer.

If you ask yourself open-ended questions like "How can I. . ." or "What can be done to. . . ?" you're allowing answers that will add insight and lead you to success.

For example:

- "How can I better understand the needs of my customers?"
- "What can be done to improve the quality of our service?"
- "How can we improve employee retention and productivity?"

Ray Stone was feeling very frustrated that his products and services for financial companies were not selling as quickly as he knew they should. He had trusted his intuition *and* his considerable business acumen to start his enterprise and had been successful at getting in front of decision makers for many Fortune 500 companies. The sales cycle from start to finish was simply taking too long and was costing him money.

Ray said he sat down at the couch in his office, closed his eyes, centered himself, took a deep breath, exhaled slowly, and asked simply, "What could we do to improve sales?"

I wish I could say a big booming voice from above gave me the answer! But honestly, that would have scared me half to death! Instead, I saw an image of a menu. At the top it said "A la carte." As I sat there it occurred to me that perhaps we were trying to sell a product that had too many features. Dividing the product into smaller portions made it easier to understand and wouldn't overwhelm the buyer. We implemented this idea and sales turned around dramatically within the month.

Ray's experience makes a case for the fact that intuitive answers come most easily when you're in a calm and relaxed state of mind. You don't need to take a long break. Simply put your calls on hold, shut the door, close your eyes and ask your questions!

gut truster tip

Ask yourself open-ended questions like "How can I..." or "What can be done to...?" By doing this you're allowing answers that will add insight and lead you to success.

CHAPTER 5

Time for a Gut Check

Here's something to meditate on today: When your head tells you one thing and your gut tells you another, go with your gut. Your gut knows things your head will never understand. So when you're at a crossroads where the stakes are high, learn to rely on owner's intuition. It's one of the most powerful decision-making tools we have.

SAM FROWINE, *CHARLOTTE BUSINESS JOURNAL*

Allen had a decision to make. He sat in my office looking extremely distressed for a man who had two equally enticing job offers. He had spent a sleepless night going over his pros and cons list in a desperate attempt to make the right choice. It was an important career decision for him and he didn't want to make the wrong move.

Company A offered him a significant increase in salary and benefits, an opportunity to make a difference as a leader in his field, and a geographic move that both he and his family found appealing.

Company B had been around longer, had a good reputation in this industry, and seemed to offer the potential for more stability.

It was offering an opportunity for investment in the company that could really pay off for Allen in the long run.

We discussed the offers at length, along with Allen's impressions of the companies and the people he interviewed with. The more we discussed the facts of the two positions, the more agitated he became. He was leaning toward accepting the offer from Company B largely because stability was important to his family and him, and he felt this corporation presented the best opportunity.

Something still didn't feel right, so I suggested he do something a little out of the ordinary for him — close his eyes, take a deep breath, and relax. I asked him to sit quietly for a few moments and put all the logic and facts out of his mind as best he could and simply focus on the in and out of his breath.

When he appeared to be settled, I said in a quiet voice, "Imagine that you're taking the job with Company A. Pay attention to any feelings, images, "knowings," or body sensations you have as you contemplate this decision." I waited about 30 seconds. "Next," I said, "imagine you're taking the job with Company B."

I was prepared to wait for him to process this, and he surprised me by exclaiming "Oh!" and opening his eyes. What happened? He explained that as I spoke the words "Company B," he had an immediate image of the company logo with a huge X through it accompanied by a sinking feeling.

He instantly tried to come up with some logical reasons for this response. I explained that in conducting this brief exercise we were asking for intuitive information that might assist him with his decision. This inner guidance will provide information that we may not consciously be aware of.

The imagery and feeling seemed fairly obvious to me. An X through the logo would appear to indicate "Don't go there," or at the very least that there was something wrong. The sinking feeling was also an important clue. If a decision lacks energy or vitality, it's your intuition trying to steer you away from that choice or situation. While I wasn't suggesting that Allen make a decision based entirely on this insight, he should add it to the mix of information he already had.

Allen left my office promising to call me to tell me the results of his decision making. I didn't hear from him again until several months had passed. He was lighthearted and laughing on the phone. He explained that after again examining his pros and cons list *and* listening to his intuition, he had taken the job with Company A. He described it as a real struggle because he truly wanted the stability of the other company. Here's where the story takes an interesting turn. Allen had just learned that Company B had unexpectedly filed for bankruptcy. When he heard this, he suddenly understood the information his intuition had provided. It all made sense. He was happy he had listened.

Checking with Your Gut

Have you ever had a knot in your stomach? It's a commonly accepted indicator that something is amiss. You're stressed about a decision. It's a warning of sorts.

Perhaps you're about to hire the wrong person or take your team into perilous territory. The tension in your belly is part of your intuitive physical system communicating "Danger ahead. Redirection is needed!"

Many scientists believe we have two brains. The one between our ears and the lesser known but equally important one in our gut. They communicate with each other. When your head gets upset, your stomach takes notice and vise versa.

The next time you're faced with a decision, large or small, check in with your gut. Does an option you're considering feel *off*, or *right*, in your belly?

Is your stomach tied in knots at the thought of making an offer to the person you just interviewed, or does it feel relaxed and at ease?

Here are some questions to ask:

- Is there an alternative that feels better?

- Is this the right time to make this decision? Does waiting a few hours (days, weeks, or months) feel better?
- Do I need more information before making this decision?
- Does the whole thing feel wrong? Or just part of it?
- What would make this decision feel right?

Is there a question or issue that keeps coming to mind that you've been dismissing? Pay attention to it. Bring it to your conscious awareness and check in with your gut. It may provide some valuable information about the correct course of action.

It's More Than Just the Gut

Intuition is a skill that, when practiced, can be honed to perfection. Imagine having a reliable "gut check" meter you can use each time you need to make a decision! As you've been reading this book, you may have begun to recognize the primary way you receive intuitive messages.

The term *gut feeling* is often used generically for a whole host of other body sensations. Physical sensations are a huge part of our intuitive guidance system. When I asked people to describe their gut feeling in more detail, I received a surprising variety of answers:

- A vibration through my whole body
- A mild electric zing
- Chills up and down my spine
- A warm surge of energy though my body
- A buzzing around my head
- Goosebumps on my arms
- My left knee hurts
- My stomach knots up
- Indigestion

- Generalized tension in my body that wasn't there previously
- Cold feet

There were many more answers, but suffice to say the body's owner was aware of receiving an intuitive communication.

One entrepreneur I spoke with said she was contemplating taking on a new piece of business. However, whenever she picked up the phone to dial the prospective client to say yes, she felt like "someone pulled the plug on my energy." She ended up turning the client down. Later she overheard someone at a networking event talking about this client and describing how incredibly difficult the client was to work with. "It was like my mind was telling me to go ahead. But my body was smarter."

What's Your Body Telling You?

So how do you learn to interpret these physical messages? First, simply be aware of what's going on with your own body. Think back to a successful decision you've made over the past few days. How did it feel in your body? Where did you feel it? How would you describe the sensation? Repeat this same set of questions with an unsuccessful decision.

Example #1: You've got a sales call to make. You've been dreading this call all morning. At around 11:30 you feel an odd surge of energy in your body and decide to pick up the phone and make the call. It turns out you reached the client at just the right time, and she was happy to hear from you.

Example #2: You wake up on Tuesday morning. The thought that I should get into the office early today pops into your mind. You override this idea by telling yourself you'll work late instead. You notice your stomach hurts.

As you pull out onto the highway, you hear the traffic reporter for your radio station announce major delays on your route to work. If you had left 30 minutes earlier, you would have avoided it all.

Begin to check in with your body when making small decisions.

- Whom should I call to get background on this issue?
- Is this a good time to make that phone call?
- Is it important for me to be at that meeting?
- Which restaurant should I choose?
- Should I work with Joe or Mary on this project?
- Which book would be most helpful in getting up to speed on this topic?

It might be a good idea to keep a journal of your decisions. What was the decision? How did it feel in your body? Was it a good, bad, or neutral decision? When you become comfortable with the way you receive insight on small decisions, you'll be surprised at the speed with which you'll be able to get accurate intuitive information on larger decisions.

gut truster tip

The next time you're faced with a decision, large or small, check in with your gut. Does an option you're considering feel *off,* or *right,* in your belly?

CHAPTER 6

Your Inner Consultant Wants a Meeting

Your Inner CEO can help you generate income streams, create opportunities, find people, build your business, maximize your profits, increase your income, solve problems, and improve your quality of life in ways you can't even imagine now.

— ROBERT SHEINFELD, AUTHOR OF *THE 11 TH ELEMENT*

David Becker is president of Philippe Becker Design (PBD), a branding and packaging agency founded in 1998. PBD was recently named the fifth fastest growing company in San Francisco and its clients include Disney, Forbes, Gap, Safeway, T-Mobile, Whole Foods Market, and Williams-Sonoma, Inc. Becker's a big fan of trusting his intuition—his "Inner Consultant." In fact he credits doing so with saving his company from a costly mistake:

We were in dire need of a key financial person for our rapidly growing firm. This was a major hire for us that would enable us to get to the next level of growth. We'd spent a great deal of time searching for the right person. Obviously they needed to be a good fit in terms of credentials. But it was also important to us that whoever we hired be an equally good fit for our culture, beliefs, and business approach.

The person we homed in on seemed to meet all the major criteria. Everything clicked. Everyone was in agreement. Frankly, I was so desperate to get that person on board I was like a kid who wants a bike for Christmas. That's how great the desire was to hire him and get him started.

At the same time I began to recognize that something was gnawing at me about this person. I can only describe it as a danger signal. Something at the back of my mind kept niggling at me. This was someone who would have access to all of our financial information. It was an extremely important position in my company, and everyone was looking to me to be the final decision maker.

I began to realize I didn't have my emotions in check about this key decision. I was a little too excited. That was part of the warning for me. I decided to do a routine background check via the Internet. Somewhat to my surprise, nothing untoward showed up about this man. Yet I still didn't feel right

I decided to go through a process that I learned while getting my MBA. I separated the decision making into three different segments. The first was my logical analysis of this person's viability. Second was my emotional state about wanting him to be the right hire. Third was my raw, unadulterated intuition. When I was able to take out the emotion and logic, I was able to see that something was still wrong.

I realized that I had allowed emotion to overpower my gut feelings. That combined with the excitement of thinking I had found the right person and having his credentials check out. After this exercise I was still left with a sense of unease. I decided to spend several thousand dollars to do a more thorough background investigation. I received the results several days later. They confirmed my instincts. He had been convicted of several felonious acts involving company funds in another state. Hiring him would have been a disaster.

The process David ultimately used to make his decision brings to mind a quote by English mystery writer Margery Allingham. She writes about one of her characters: "He did not arrive at this conclusion by the decent process of quiet, logical deduction, nor yet by the blinding flash of glorious intuition, but by the shoddy, untidy process halfway between the two by which one usually gets to know things."

Questions for the Inner Consultant

There is part of you that knows the best direction toward success in any endeavor. Write questions you would like to ask your "Inner Consultant."

You may find the responses come easily if you sit quietly for a few minutes. Others have found it best to sit at their keyboard and simply write whatever comes to mind. The intuitive answers may also come to you when you least expect them!

Make a statement about what you want and then ask an open-ended question. Here are some ideas to get you started:

- "I'd like to create record-breaking sales this quarter. What is the best way to do this?"
- "I want to motivate my product development team. What's a good approach?"
- "I want to feel excited by my career again. What are some options that would work for me?"
- "I'd like to improve my ability to listen to my intuition. What steps should I take?"

Look at your answers from time to time and see how the intuitive intelligence you received has shifted your thoughts in new directions.

A colleague of mine had an interesting variation on the above method. He was a decidedly "low-tech" kind of guy. He wrote a question to his Inner Consultant on a 3 x 5 card every morning. He kept the card in his shirt pocket. He explains that throughout the day, he writes flashes of insight, "thought messages," and coincidences relevant to his question. He feels that having them in his pocket keeps him attuned to the questions and open to the answers.

I ran into him recently at a speech I gave. He showed me a stack of his cards that represented several days' worth of inquiry. They were filled with creative information and wisdom that he credits with helping him increase sales, hire good employees, and successfully resolve a difficult issue with one of his biggest clients. "I couldn't survive without my cards. They're my second brain!" he said with a laugh.

Your Inner Consultant is the creative part of your mind that answers when you ask questions such as "I wonder how else I can look at this problem?" Or "I wonder how else I could deal with this decision?" Or "I wonder what other possibilities exist to solve this problem?"

A Meeting with the Inner Consultant

Jean, the president and CEO of the service company mentioned in Chapter 2, described a wonderful Inner Consultant type of exercise she created and used at the annual retreat for her senior executive staff.

On the morning of the first day of the three-day retreat, Jean addressed her group, acknowledging that they'd had a difficult year. She said she had a great deal of confidence in them and that her intention was to use the retreat to address their concerns as well as to come up with creative solutions.

In front of each person she had placed a 5 x 8 card. On one side it simply said, "My question for the expert." She told the 16 people present that tomorrow she would be introducing them to an authority in their field. That person wanted to see the questions beforehand as a way of preparing for their meeting.

Jean asked that they give some thought to the subject, and to help them focus she played some meditative music. At the end of five minutes she collected their cards and proceeded with the scheduled events for the day.

The next morning she announced that the expert who was to meet with them was experiencing a delay and would join them shortly. In anticipation of his arrival, she read a list of his accomplishments. They included

- the many years he'd been in the industry,
- the large number of awards his company had received,
- the accolades written about him in the press, and
- the philanthropic work he'd been involved with.

"Since he isn't here, I'd like to distribute the questions you wrote yesterday and ask that you simply make sure you don't end up with your own question." Then she added, "Perhaps while we're waiting we could get in touch with our own inner expert and discuss how we might answer these questions."

With the meditation music playing once again in the background, Jean asked them to close their eyes, take a few deep, centering breaths, and ask themselves the question that was in front of them. "I want you to take your time. Simply pay attention to any words or phrases that come to your mind, any feelings that arise in answer to this question and any knowing you have. When you're ready, write your responses on the back of the card."

After about five minutes of observing her staff with their eyes closed, there was a flurry of activity. Pens in hand, people were bent over their cards, writing their answers. After everyone finished, Jean collected the cards and they took a break. When they returned, she announced, "It occurs to me that in this room we have a great deal of business acumen and experience. In fact, all the things that I previously read about this 'expert' are true of the people gathered here. I have a confession to make. The true expert I was expecting today was each of you and your accumulated wisdom."

With that, Jean once again distributed the cards, this time with their answers on the back. She asked each individual one by one to stand and read the question as well as the answer. "It was incredibly powerful, moving, and bonding. We were all struck by the heartfelt concerns raised by each member of the team as well as by the profound answers.

"What moved all of us was the unadorned wisdom that resonated throughout all the responses. It was 'Care about each other.' That was it, pure and simple. I closed by reminding everyone that we all get stuck sometimes. We get confused and overwhelmed by our personal and business lives. Yet within each one of us there resides a spirit that knows the answer."

gut truster tip

Your Inner Consultant is the creative part of your mind that answers when you ask questions such as "I wonder how else I can look at this problem?" Or "I wonder how else I could deal with this decision?" Or "I wonder what other possibilities exist to solve this problem?"

CHAPTER 7

A Day in the Life of a Business Intuitive

*Ask some people what they based a decision on and they might say, "Gut instinct."
But would they be willing to base a major business decision on that instinct?
Perhaps they'd be more comfortable relying on someone who bases her profession
on that instinct. That would be Lynn A. Robinson, a business intuitive who
runs Intuitive Consulting Inc., where the gut instinct can help keep firms from
going belly up.*

— FROM "IN SYNC WITH INSTINCT," *METROWEST DAILY NEWS*

There was a message left on my voice mail on a Monday morning after the above article about my business intuitive services had appeared in the *MetroWest Daily News*. "I've read about you and understand you might be able to help us solve a problem we're facing. Would you be available on Wednesday afternoon to meet with us? We need to make a decision soon."

When I returned the call to Michael Olson, he explained further. He was the CEO for a leading software company. I had a new product whose scheduled release date was less than three months away, and there was an "issue" with one of the senior IT employees. It would cost the company hundreds of thousands of dollars in lost revenue to replace the man at this point. To hire someone new and get him or her up to speed in time to meet the deadline was just not possible.

Mr. Olson was straightforward. "I don't understand what you do or how you do it. I don't really care to know. If you can help us get some insight into what's going on with this employee that enables him to get back on track, it's worth gold to me right now."

What about Bob?

On Wednesday morning I rang the buzzer of the door to the restored factory building that served as the software company's headquarters. Olson answered the door himself and ushered me into the large conference room that featured huge windows looking out to a beautiful pond. Instead of the private meeting I had imagined, Olson introduced me to the president, the comptroller, and the human resources manager. Clearly this issue was a major concern for the company.

I noted with some amusement that they all seemed relieved that I was "normal." I was dressed in a dark business suit and carried a leather briefcase. No turban. No crystal ball. No incense or invoking of spirits. No woo-woo.

I explained how I work. I call my service "Intuitive Consulting." I provide critical intelligence, intuitively gained, that provides executives and entrepreneurs with insight that enables them to resolve tough problems.

I want to receive only a *brief* overview of the problem and the name of the person they were concerned about. I do not want to hear their opinions or ideas on what's wrong or what they have tried or not tried in order to remedy the situation. I don't want their information to influence the insight I receive intuitively.

"Bob is our senior IT person. He's the main person responsible for the success of our new software. He has almost impossible-to-replace knowledge of our company and our unique niche industry. He's managing a group of ten people. In the past few months he's been "off"—not following through properly. We don't know what's wrong or how to fix it. We're desperate. We can't afford to hire someone else at this late stage of our new product development."

That was the extent of the input. I close my eyes. I find it helpful to do this because it allows me to concentrate more efficiently on the often ephemeral intuitive information I receive. I'm also able to avoid picking up on nonintuitive clues like body language and facial expressions. I take a deep breath and allow myself to internally retreat from the state of high anxiety in the room. I form a series of questions in my mind.

- "Is there anything going on in the company I should be aware of?"
- "Is there anything going on in the team that I should be aware of?"
- "What's going on with Bob?"
- "What could they do to help Bob?"
- "Is there a problem with the software?"
- "What can I say or do that will be helpful to this company?"

While the questions above and the intuitive answers I received below look as though they'd take a long time to process, they actually came to me almost instantaneously. The best analogy I can use is that of an Internet search engine. It's as if I Google the name of the company and immediately receive information about it, the bio of its founder, its mission, the description of its products, and so on. Much like a search engine, the more specific I am in my query, the more precise the response I receive.

The question that has the most charge around it is "What's going on with Bob?" I decide to start there. As I form the question in my mind, I begin to receive information instantaneously through images, feelings, words, knowing. The information is fleeting. It passes through my inner sensory system quickly, and I find if I don't write it down or speak it, it can disappear like a dream drifting away when you awaken from a deep sleep.

About Bob:

- Words: Eager. Quick. Likes the company. Bright. Likes his job. Capable. Loyal.
- Feelings: Confused. Overwhelmed. Besieged.
- Symbolic images: A meeting in this boardroom. Words seem to be flying around the room. I note that they appear to be flying over Bob's head. People are feverishly writing notes. The meeting ends, and a question mark appears over Bob's head.
- Knowing: A learning disorder.

I ask in my inner dialogue, "Does Bob have a learning disorder?"

- Words: Yes
- Image: Heads are nodding in affirmation.

I ask, "What would help?"

- Words: Assign someone to him. Debrief.
- Image: See someone (an outside consultant?) who takes notes. This person will be assigned to Bob and debrief him one-on-one after the meeting.

Is there anything else I need to know right now?

- Silence. I don't receive any images, feelings, or the like.

Only about 15 seconds have passed. I open my eyes. Everyone is staring at me expectantly.

"I think Bob has a learning disability. He doesn't seem able to process information properly, especially when he's hearing it in a tense meeting environment. He's a very bright guy. He likes working here. He's very committed to the company and the product."

I pause. As I'm saying the above, I receive what feels like a "thought balloon." The words are simply "three months ago."

I continue by asking, "Did you make a shift three months ago from one-on-one meetings with Bob to the group input you're currently doing?"

Everyone looks at each other and nods.

"Is that when the concerns about Bob began?"

Again they say yes.

"I think that's the problem. Because of the way Bob processes information, he has a great deal of difficulty in these meetings. He doesn't appear to come away with a concrete to-do list as you imagine he would. He seems to get what everyone is saying but then doesn't translate it to 'here's what I need to do in order to make this happen.' I'd like to suggest you assign someone to debrief him by himself after the meeting and provide the written notes. If you do that, he'll be back to the old Bob, and your product will come out on time."

That was it. They filled me in on more details of what had happened and what they had already done to try to solve the problem. I'm struck by the number of executive hours that had previously been devoted to the "Bob problem." Our entire intuitive insight meeting took about 15 minutes.

After 20 years of doing this kind of work, I still can't say I totally understand how these insights come to me. However, I left the office feeling pretty good about all that had transpired and walked confidently to where I had parked my car. It was only then that I realized I had mistakenly walked out of the building from a different exit and was lost in the wrong parking lot. Go figure!

Two months later I was called back to the client's office to help provide insight on another issue. The words "You nailed it with Bob. Your recommendation totally solved the problem," rang in my ears.

Honing Your Intuition

Could anyone receive the information the way I do with my clients? The short answer is yes. The longer answer is that I believe each of us has a gift we're born with. For me, it is a gift for intuition. For some, it may be an extraordinary musical talent; for another, it could be a remarkable athletic ability. Yet someone else could be gifted with a natural fluency in language.

Could the rest of us average folks learn to be good at music, sports, or languages? Of course we could—with practice, interest, and diligence. The same is true for the "intuitive skill." It's what this book is all about. My intention is to help you hone the innate intuitive abilities you already have and get so good at it you can call on it to help you solve even the thorniest business challenges.

Where do you begin? Keep a small notebook or PDA with you at all times. Get into the habit of asking your intuition questions and writing down the answers you receive. This practice has multiple benefits:

- By asking your intuition questions and writing the answers, you've begun developing your intuitive muscles.
- You'll have a record of your intuitive answers to refer back to as needed. Often these insights may make more sense with a little hindsight.
- It will also give you confidence in your abilities as you see the correct answers add up in your notebook.
- As with developing any skill, you may not be right 100 percent of the time. Keeping track of the information will help you recognize when you're on target and when you're off target.

Intuition often comes in fragments of information similar to pieces of a puzzle. As you jot impressions in your book, you may find the puzzle comes together, enabling you to see the whole picture much more quickly.

Just begin. It doesn't need to be difficult. Intuition is the right side of your brain, creative inspiration stuff. Have fun with it!

gut truster tip

Keep an intuition journal. By asking your intuition questions and writing the answers, you've begun developing your intuitive muscles.

CHAPTER 8

Take an Insight Break

I learned that inspiration does not come like a bolt, nor is it kinetic,
energetic striving, but it comes into us slowly and quietly and all the time,
though we must regularly and every day give it a little chance to start flowing,
prime it with a little solitude and idleness.

— BRENDA UELAND, WRITER

We're often so swept up in our professional roles that we rush from meeting to phone call to e-mail and back again, and we don't take time for even a brief break. However, I believe that reverie is crucial to the intuitive mind. I found clear evidence of this while writing this very chapter. I had nailed the beginning, and had come up with the story you'll read below. I then found myself staring at the page, editing the same sentence over and over. The dreaded writer's block!

I decided to go for a walk and simply ask my creative mind, "What do I need to write for this chapter?" By the time I'd completed a stroll around my neighborhood, I had several solid ideas that seemed worthy to write about. (I hope you'll agree.)

Take a Hike

When you're overwhelmed and feeling stymied and blocked, making yourself work harder is usually counterproductive. Your creativity dries up; the numbers you're trying to crunch swim before your eyes. The intuitive insight you need just isn't coming to you. The solution? When you're besieged and need answers, take a hike.

Is there a place near your office that makes you feel calm? Go there the next time you need insight. The answers you receive during those 30 minutes will be more than equal to the hours of statistics and analysis you had planned.

When you get there, begin to stroll. Focus on the present. Use all your senses and take in all that is around you. Notice the fragrance in the air, the sounds of the birds, and the breeze on your skin. Take some slow, deep breaths. Observe how you feel.

As you become calmer, think about what has been disturbing your peace of mind. Frame it into a question as you continue your walk and listen for answers.

Intuitive insights come to you more easily when you're relaxed and have an open state of mind. Ask questions. . . The answers will come.

Saba Alhadi decided to take this kind of break when she was trying to determine the best "next steps" for her career. She said:

> The idea for my business began on a leisurely stroll on an unusually warm December day in 2001. I was admiring the architecture and the beauty of the city near Boston Common. With my camera at hand, I started taking creative pictures of the scenes around me.
>
> Then, inspiration struck! I thought, "What if I combine my photography knowledge and teaching skills with Boston history and create a walking tour business with photography tips?" I knew right then and there I had my

business idea. I didn't waver from my goal from that moment on. Lots of research and hard work followed that momentous day.

I turned my business idea into a reality: Photo Walks was launched on May 1, 2002, with only two tours. Today, four tours are offered. Since then, I have received extensive media attention and have written a book called Boston in Photographs. *Little did I know that a stroll would lead to meeting a lot of great people, having an impact on how they take pictures, and a lot of adventures!*

Many of the people I interviewed for this book mentioned taking a brief walk near their office as a way to both take a break and receive inspiration.

Other Kinds of Breaks

Here are some other ways interviewees invoke intuitive insight at work:

- I subscribe to an "inspirational quote" e-newsletter. I print out a quote and post it where I can view it throughout the day. It helps keep me focused on what life is all about.
- Before I start my day I read a verse from the Bible or other inspirational book.
- I make it a priority to eat lunch in a nearby park or, in inclement weather, even in my car. I find after I return to my desk I have a huge burst of creativity.
- I go to the gym for a half hour during my workday. Working out gets the cobwebs out of my brain, and I come up with wonderful ideas while running on the treadmill or lifting weights.
- My company has a meditation room. I go there for reflection and prayer as part of my lunch break. I come back to work feeling centered and relaxed. The answers to issues I

was struggling with in the morning seem to be resolved during that brief time for contemplation.

- If I can't actually get away from the office, I make a point of changing my location. It can often be as simple as switching from my desk to the couch in my office. The minor change helps me maintain my mental alertness and increases my productivity. I actually think of it as my "inspiration couch."

- I bring my laptop to the park. Nothing like a change of scenery to fire up my creative juices.

- I reserve time in our company conference room several times a week. It looks out to a huge field filled with wildflowers. I use those occasions as my intuition time. I bring a notepad, colored pens, and pencils and do some creative mind-mapping. I get amazing results fast.

The "intuitive break" strategy I heard echoed most often was from those who confessed they took a nap at work. Surprisingly, a vast majority of executives and entrepreneurs alike confessed that it was one of the quickest ways they found to make a decision or come up with a solution.

Take a Power Nap

According to Dr. Sara Mednick, a research scientist at the prestigious Salk Institute for Biological Studies in La Jolla, California, the benefits of even a brief 20-minute nap are profound. Studies show naps result in greater alertness, improved memory retention, and creative insight.

There's evidence that many companies are catching on to the idea of napping in the workplace. Some of these include Union Pacific Railroad, Ben and Jerry's, and Levi Strauss — all providing "spent tents" (nap lounges) for their employees. There's even a company called "MetroNaps" that leases "nap pods" to businesses with sleep-deprived employees.

Yarde Metals Inc. in Southington, Connecticut, is a metals distribution company that built a 2,000-square-foot "nap room" in each of its facilities. Each of them is large enough to accommodate 20 employees at a time.

Accounting firm Deloitte Consulting in Pittsburgh has designed a special "napnasium" for the comfort of their employees. It is open to any employee needing rest and has recliners and blinds. The company made *Fortune* magazine's list of the best 100 U.S. companies to work for in 2003, so its enlightened attitude toward napping seems to be reaping rewards.

Kansas City–based architectural firm Gould Evans Goodman Associates pitched three "spent tents" in a corner of its office— each outfitted with air mattress, sleeping bag, foam pad, flannel pillow, Walkman, eye shades, and alarm clock. According to the company spokesperson, Mindy Highfill, "When it's the middle of the afternoon and I'm not getting work done because I'm tired, I know I'm better off taking a 10- to 15-minute nap," she says. "Then, when I go back to work, I'm refreshed and revitalized and able to get a lot more done."

If you're concerned that taking a nap will give the impression that you're a slacker, just take a look at legendary people who swore by these power naps.

Winston Churchill used to plan his strategic meetings around his naptime. "You must sleep sometime between lunch and dinner, and no halfway measures. Take off your clothes and get into bed. That's what I always do. Don't think you will be doing less work because you sleep during the day. That's a foolish notion held by people who have no imaginations. You will be able to accomplish more. You get two days in one—well, at least one and a half."

American Presidents Ronald Reagan and Bill Clinton were famous for their naps. And John F. Kennedy was often seen taking 15-minute naps by leaning back and putting his forearm over his face.

Albert Einstein used to take afternoon naps to recuperate and was quoted many times on his thoughts about how naps increased his productivity, creativity, and intuition.

Brahms napped at the piano while he composed his famous lullaby.

Thomas Edison, the inventor of the electric light, used to take frequent naps during the day instead of sleeping at night.

Dr. David Dinges, a sleep researcher at the University of Pennsylvania, is a strong advocate of prophylactic napping, taking what he and others call a "power nap" during the day to head off the cumulative effects of sleep loss. He explained that the brain "sort of sputters" when it is deprived of sufficient sleep, causing slips in performance and attentiveness.

Dr. James Maas, a Cornell University psychologist and author of *Power Sleep*, agrees, pointing out that naps "greatly strengthen the ability to pay close attention to details and to make critical decisions."

We may be facing the day when your place of work actually encourages you—as my kindergarten teacher did—to "put your heads down on your desks and rest a while." When you see the boost in creativity and productivity—*and* your intuition—you'll be glad you did!

gut truster tip

Get away from your office and take a brief creativity break. It's one of the quickest ways to make a decision or come up with a solution to a thorny problem.

CHAPTER 9

What Fires You Up?

It is always with excitement that I wake up in the morning wondering
what my intuition will toss up to me, like gifts from the sea. I work with it
and rely on it. It's my partner.

— JONAS SALK, INVENTOR OF THE POLIO VACCINE

Shira Miller is president of Shira Miller Communications, Inc. Her passion and enthusiasm fairly crackle through the phone lines as I talk with her at her boutique public relations agency in Atlanta. She loves her work and finds that intuition is one of the most powerful tools she uses to run her business:

I've learned that my gut is a lot smarter than my brain in assessing new
business opportunities. For me, the intuitive information arrives almost in the
form of a visual "thought bubble" in my brain (like in the comic strips). I can
hear "this is right," "go for it," "watch out, there could be a problem." Most of
the time I listen to it, but problems always arise when I don't.

A year ago, I had the opportunity to handle all aspects of an event called the
"Search for Atlanta's Funniest Accountant." It was for a local financial
recruiting firm called Accountants One. This was a different animal from the

typical strategic corporate PR work I handle, but my internal thought balloon lit up like a pinball machine. I knew I wanted it 100 percent and kept receiving intuitive messages like "this is fantastic," and "this will be wonderful and challenging"–even before I met the potential client or knew what kind of money was involved.

So I pulled out all the stops to pitch the business and I got it. Handling this event has been one of my favorite assignments ever. We adore the client, who is extremely ethical and a pleasure to work with. We ran all aspects of the Funniest Accountant Search and it was a huge success. The venue sold out in four days, we secured publicity ranging from a front-page story in the Atlanta Journal & Constitution *to the* Wall Street Journal *and made great strides in raising our client's visibility. And now we're going to handle all marketing communications for Accountants One while preparing to do the event again next year.*

Her logical mind told her this piece of business wasn't the right one for her. Her intuition shouted "Go for it!"

Enthusiasm

The word *enthusiasm* comes from the Greek root *entheos*, meaning *God within* or *guidance within*. Whether you call it enthusiasm, passion, interest, zest, vitality, energy, or even lightness, it provides an important clue whenever you're trying to make a decision.

It makes sense on some very logical level to pay attention to your enthusiasm. Whether you're thinking about a career change, a hiring decision, or working with a certain client. Simply put, if something feels exciting or has a lot of vitality, it's an indication from your intuition about the direction to follow. Conversely, if a decision makes you feel drained, bored, or enervated, it's a strong signal to move away from that choice.

This sense of enthusiasm is most *critically* important when you're contemplating a change in career direction. Brian Rullo had been an agent in the life insurance field for over 30 years. He consistently won awards from his company as one of the top ten agents in the country. He was making a great living, had the acknowledgment of his company and respect from peers, and his clients loved him.

Life was bliss, right? That's what Brian kept telling himself every morning when he got out of bed. "I should be happy. I've achieved everything I ever wanted. What more is there?" Yet he couldn't shake the feeling of malaise he had begun to experience almost a year earlier at an awards ceremony honoring him for his achievements. "Here I was at the top of my game and I felt like s—. It got so bad, I even talked to my doctor about getting on antidepressants. And I'm the quintessential optimist! Everyone who knows me knows I'm up, positive, cheerful. The glass is always half full for me."

He remembers picking up the book *Managing Upside Down* by Tom Chapell, the CEO and cofounder of Tom's of Maine. A phrase leapt out at him. It was one of the seven "intentions" mentioned by Chapell to help managers achieve far-reaching results. "Envision your destiny! Imagine your future with your head and your heart," it read.

Brian said he had never before thought of himself as a cocreator of his life. "I had a job. I was good at it. I made decent money. I provided a high-quality service. That was who I was. I had followed the path of least resistance in my life and had the good fortune to have it work out. Now it wasn't. Life just felt boring. I'd lost my passion. That phrase encouraging me to 'envision my destiny' got me fired up! I began to examine my values with particular attention to where I felt a glimmer of enthusiasm and vitality."

Brian decided to accelerate the process of self-discovery by working with me to help him follow his intuition to a new career. As he diligently worked on the idea of a new vocation, he saw he could integrate many of the aptitudes he possessed that had made him successful and reconfigure them in a new career.

I asked him to put aside for now the question of *how* he would implement his choices. That would come later. I explained that often people put the cart before the horse; they try to decide *how* they're going to achieve something before fully deciding what they really want. By doing that, they usually manage to talk themselves out of whatever initially excited them. The phrase "that's just not realistic" has doomed many an intuitive impulse right from the start.

Vitality Meter

Following is a list of questions I asked Brian to think about as he reflected on various vocational options. You may want to get your notebook and write down the answers for yourself. This technique works for a variety of issues. It doesn't need to be a career-focused concern. Try it out when you're making your next hiring decision. Or as Shira Miller did at the start of the chapter, use the technique to identify the right client to pursue:

- Think of the options you have before you. List at least six in your notebook.
- Which one(s) are you drawn to?
- Is there one that leaps to your attention?
- Do one or more of the choices feel draining or enervating?
- Do you feel a sense of excitement about one over the others?
- Is there a visceral response you receive about pursuing this course of action? (A physical sensation is one of the ways that intuition communicates.)
- What action do you feel most enthusiastic about? That's the right direction to follow.

Brian listed his options as follows. I included his notes in parentheses to give you an idea about how this works.

1. Stay in my present job until I retire. (No energy there. Makes me want to go to sleep.)

2. Take some courses at the local college in psychology or a similar topic. (That reaches about a 4 on the vitality meter. Not high enough!)

3. Take a year off and hope that at the end of that time I'll have it all figured out. (That makes me much too nervous and I'd drive my wife crazy.)

4. Work part-time at my current job and explore options around starting a sales-training business. (That one gets the vitality meter hitting high marks!)

5. Investigate becoming a life coach and help other business-people explore career change. (That scores a 5 on a scale of 1 to 10. I'm concerned that talking with people about problems isn't my forte. I'm also not very patient.)

6. Look into joining the National Speakers Association and/or Toastmasters to uncover ways to make a living as a trainer/consultant in sales. (Definitely excited about this.)

After going over this list and discussing it with his wife and several trusted friends, Brian decided his vitality meter was pointing him in the direction of creating his own sales-training business. Numbers 4 and 6 were the indicators for him. The thought of completely leaving his current job didn't feel right for now. Fortunately he was able to negotiate staying in insurance sales part-time. That gave him both an income cushion and some structure that felt comfortable to him.

I received an e-mail from Brian several months ago. It read, "The vitality meter was right! I have four contracts for sales training this month alone. It's amazing how when you're on the right track, business just comes to you!"

gut truster tip

When you're trying to make a decision, write down your options. As you review the list, notice how you respond. Which option scores the highest on your "inner vitality meter?"

CHAPTER 10

Your Higher Power at Work

Listen to me; keep silent, and I will teach you wisdom.

— JOB 33:33

Intuition is a ready source of direction—a compass of the soul—available to all of us. It's an invisible intelligence that animates our world and provides wisdom to guide our life. When we follow its wisdom, it invariably leads us to success and happiness in both our personal and business life.

I've often joked that it would be wonderful to arrive in this world with an instruction manual that gives us step-by-step directions for living a full and happy life as well as for succeeding in business. Over the years I've come to understand that we do in fact receive this guidance. We're hardwired for this source of wisdom through our intuition.

Fortunately, we all have the ability to tap into this power. We are all capable of developing it for practical use in everyday life as well as for discovering and achieving life goals. Many people think of it as the domain of a gifted few, even though intuition is now recognized not as a rare, accidental talent but as a natural skill that all of us can cultivate.

Connecting with Your Spirit

Learning to trust your gut at work is much more than simply paying attention to your hunches. It involves looking within for the answers, living life with courage, faith, patience, and trust. It also involves connecting with your spirit through daily practice and taking action on the wisdom you receive.

Connecting with your spirit at work is apparently good for business as well. A study by the highly respected Wilson Learning Company found that 39 percent of the variability in corporate performance is attributable to the personal satisfaction of the staff. Spirituality was cited as the second most important factor in personal happiness (after health) by the majority of Americans questioned in a USA Weekend poll, with 47 percent saying that spirituality was the most important element of their happiness.

I believe there is a wise, loving, and creative intelligence that we are all part of. It guides our thoughts, provides inspired ideas, and connects us to each other. Many of the people I interviewed for this book felt strongly that their intuition comes from a spiritual source. They argued that hunches and instinct weren't simply pattern recognition or awareness of subconscious information. They alluded to intuition more as a sixth sense or the proverbial "still, quiet, inner voice" that unites them to their higher self.

Each person had a unique way of describing this "invisible intelligence." They called it by different names: God, wisdom within, universal intelligence, or simply a higher consciousness.

Ken MacDonald, an electrical systems engineer put it this way:

> Quantum physics has been telling us for hundreds of years that we simply cannot explain certain things. Our human pride tells us: (1) If I can't see it, it isn't there. (2) If I can't do it, it can't be done. (3) If I can't explain it, it can't be true. Sixth-sense awareness is out there for everyone. It's up to each of us to be open to this consciousness.

Nancy Baker, a senior executive at a major academic medical center, told me she views her business relationships as a way to practice spirituality in action. She combines this belief with a strong reliance on intuition to assist her in gaining insight about the people she works with:

> *I see business as an opportunity to engage with a wide variety of people to make good things happen. I often think that difficult people are thrown in my path to challenge me to remember that life is all about creating things, stuff, ideas, or whatever that serve humanity.*
>
> *I've learned through my work that staying focused on a positive vision and looking at my coworkers with compassion, no matter how they're behaving, keeps me centered and able to motivate people toward doing the right thing. It's not always easy, but offering compassion is a very disarming and effective management tool.*
>
> *Using intuition to try to "divine" why people may be behaving in an aggressive or defensive manner has really helped me get through some tough roadblocks and get people to act as a team to get things done.*

Guidance through Prayer

Prayer is the primary way we talk to God about our concerns. I believe that intuition is one of the ways God answers. A thought may pop into your mind. The person with the answer to your problem may coincidentally walk into your office. Or you may act on an impulse to turn on the radio at just the right time to hear someone provide an insight you need.

Asking for guidance through prayer is something easily done at work. Nancy, the medical center senior executive describes how prayer provided a creative solution to an issue she had been struggling with for weeks:

> *I was putting together a high-stakes strategic planning retreat for 150 senior physicians and executives. My challenge: I needed to figure out how to get them to actively participate and share their ideas at the retreat.*
>
> *After thinking about it for days, I put my head down on my desk and prayed for the answer. The idea just popped into my head: Put them in a learning*

environment just outside their comfort zone, where they will feel compelled to perform for a luminary's approval.

I wrote the information up as if it were a Harvard Business School [HBS] case study. We asked one of our board members, a charismatic HBS professor, to "teach" the case at the retreat. I had the hotel ballroom set up as an HBS classroom. The physicians and executives were all so stimulated by the setting and the exciting group dynamic that we actually had to cut off discussion when we ran out of time.

A few years later, the retreat is still thought of as the most interesting and engaging meeting of its kind. As for the idea that made it such a success, I think of it as my own case study of intuition at work.

More Ways to Connect with Your Spirit at Work

What are some other ways to connect with your spirit at work?

Take a Nature Break

Take a few moments to step outside, rain or shine, and go for a short walk. You may see an unusual cloud formation or a resilient weed pressing up through the pavement, feel inspired by the birds soaring in the sky, hear a child's laugh, or be especially appreciative of the clean air you breathe. Simply being away from your desk may be enough to open your mind to some creative and innovative solutions.

Focus on Gratitude

We spend much of our life waiting, whether it's for a taxi, for the elevator to take us to our office, for a meeting to begin, or for the traffic to move during rush hour. When you find yourself with a few moments on your hands, think silent thoughts of gratitude for all that you have.

Spirituality.com surveyed more than 1,000 people on this topic. Over 74 percent express gratitude by openly displaying a positive attitude through written or verbal expressions of thanks, praying, volunteering, or acknowledging a higher power for the good in their life. "These findings speak volumes about the state of the human spirit," said Chris Raymond, spirituality.com executive editor and general manager. "Something as simple and natural as feeling and living gratitude can be the essential spiritual ingredient for improving any situation, and lead to an overall happier, healthier life."

Learn to Meditate

Don't just do something. . . sit there! Companies as diverse as McKinsey, Deutsche Bank, Hughes Aircraft, Yahoo! and Apple are all getting in on the meditation bandwagon. They're being won over, in part, by findings at the National Institutes of Health, the University of Massachusetts, and the Mind/Body Medical Institute at Harvard University, all of whom conclude that meditation increases brainwave activity, enhances intuition, and improves concentration.

Ask Your Intuition

The next time you find yourself fraught with anxiety, check in with your higher self. Get in the habit of asking questions of your intuition and expecting a reply. You might ask, "What could I do to feel calmer about the meeting this afternoon?" In response, you get an image of a quiet lunch in the park by your office. That's one of the ways your intuition responds—through images. Your intuition is connected to a higher wisdom that always knows what you need and provides the answers to even the toughest problems.

gut truster tip

Intuition is an invisible intelligence that animates our world and provides wisdom to guide our life. Take small moments throughout your day to simply check in with your inner guidance.

CHAPTER 11

Develop an Intuitive Creative Team

Creativity in the workplace must be nurtured and cultivated for it to flourish. This means creating a culture of trust and having the freedom to express new ideas without being ridiculed, allowing room for mistakes, and developing the radar to spot opportunities in unexpected places. Many of the inventions that are now commonplace, such as 3M's Post-It notes, started out as "mistakes."

— LINDA NAIMAN, AUTHOR OF *ORCHESTRATING COLLABORATION AT WORK*

Jan Hills helps human resources professionals trust their intuition. In fact, the tag line for her business, Hills Consultancy in Surrey, England, is "Developing HR People With Guts!" She explains that over the many years she's worked as a consultant, she's observed, "There are people in every company who always seem to get it right. They make more money for you than most, and they're a big reason your company is successful."

She devised a system she calls "The Success Profile" that helps understand the secrets of the company's outstanding salespeople. Jan described working with a luxury goods retailer with stores in the United States, Europe, and Asia and with headquarters in Italy.

She discovered that the salespeople with the best customer service had three distinct characteristics that set them apart from the average salesperson:

1. They truly cared about the customer, not just about making the sale.
2. They were very goal oriented. They worked hard, visualized their success, and set high standards for themselves.
3. If they had a difficult customer, they could bounce back quickly by using a positive internal dialog. In other words, they could control their own state of mind.

Jan also created a success profile for human resources managers.

The human resource group was unusual in that they already highly valued their intuition as a decision-making tool. My task was to help them develop this skill so they could rely on it as a quick and effective way to hire the right people in an easy and effortless manner.

I prepared for my training with them by assembling a set of photographs of a wide variety of individuals along with a description of their backgrounds and biographies. At my training session, I put the photos up on the wall and asked the managers to write down their impressions of the talents, skills, strengths, and weaknesses of the people in the pictures.

I encouraged them to pay particular attention to how they received this information. Did it come as an image, a feeling, a word or phrase, a physical sensation? I gave them about 30 minutes to complete this exercise.

At the end of that time, we discussed in detail the insights they had perceived about each of the individuals in the photos. When we had completed this part with everyone in the room, I brought out the background/bio pages and read the corresponding descriptions. It was absolutely amazing how accurate they had been!

To give you a sense of this, I had thrown in a photo of a very nice-looking young man who had, in fact, been convicted of a series of kidnappings. Without knowing anything yet about their colleagues' impressions, almost to a person the individuals had written about this young man things like "danger," "something wrong," and "dishonest." We were all quite astounded.

The company also created new interview forms that included a space for writing intuitive impressions about the job candidate. Jan shared with the group a technique she called "Stop the Clock."

It's basically this:

- You're introduced to the candidate and shake hands.
- Internally, create a pause and ask, "What's my first impression?"
- Jot that down in the space provided on the form.

Throughout the interview the managers had to seek evidence to *disprove* their intuition. If they found no evidence, they followed their gut reaction. If the candidate was hired, Jan encouraged the interviewer to go back to these forms after several months to see if their initial impressions were confirmed. "It was helpful for them to see that their intuitive reactions proved correct in almost all cases. As the result of this training, the recruiters became more confident, and the hiring of successful candidates increased proportionally."

I spoke with Simon Steel at his headquarters in Somerset, England. He uses his intuition to discern what his consulting clients need. He also encourages the use of it by his clients to help them choose successful business strategies:

I call my business "imageSHAPER" because these two words capture the essence of what I do and how I do it. Its success combines my 30 years of business experience with an effective use of intuition. I'll give you an example.

I recently did some work for a consultancy business. The project was kicked off with an informal dinner, during which I "tuned in" to the dynamics of my clients. I listened carefully to what they said as well as what they didn't say. I paid close attention to the body language between the partners, because in this kind of business there are often issues around the levels of effort.

After my strategic assessment phase, I facilitated a workshop in a neutral environment away from their offices. I used a highly tuned intuitive process based on visual metaphors and supporting statements, all of which led to (in their words) "a clear understanding of both the current and future opportunities" for their business.

I've used this process successfully in numerous situations involving complex issues such as a breakdown in business relationships, lack of clarity about future objectives, and an inability to define the nature and personality of a business. I'm quite certain that my effectiveness as a consultant is due in no small part to my ability to use, trust, and apply my intuition.

Intuition and Creativity

What if your company, team, or department is not as open to intuition and creativity as the groups described above? It's tough when there are individuals that resist change, and every company has them. They seem to have an aversion to any modification to the status quo and can be counted on to come up with lines like: "That won't work"; "It will cost too much"; "But that's not how we've always done it"; and accompanied by a loud sigh. . . "We *tried* that before." I call them the Creativity Killers.

Gail McMeekin, author of *The Twelve Secrets of Highly Creative Women,* explains the difference between intuition and creativity this way:

Creativity is about bringing something new into being whether it's a new solution to a problem, a new method or device, or a new art form or design.

Intuition is a powerful resource that guides people through the ups and downs of the creative process. Our intuition pulls us towards a specific project or pursuit that will point us in the direction of success.

Put another way, intuition is where your creativity lives. Intuition is guidance within us that provides direction or insight to solve problems, make decisions, and get creative. Creativity is a new way of seeing or doing something that can come about as a result of that intuitive perception.

Creativity and intuition are vitally important to the success of any business. So important, says Dr. John Kao, author of *Jamming: The Art and Discipline of Business Creativity,* that "The only kinds of companies that don't need creativity these days are companies that don't need to change."

Creativity and Intuition Boosters

How do you begin to foster creativity in your own business, team, or department? The list below will get you started! Make creativity a core value. Make it clear to your staff that intuition, creativity, and innovation are important to you and the company. Don't just pay lip service to the idea, back it up with action.

- *Talk about creativity.* How do people define it? Why is it important? What tools does your staff need in order to be creative? What do they need from you as a boss, coworker, or leader in order to be creative? What encourages creativity? What discourages it?
- *Design an inspiring work environment.* Ask your team to come up with six ways to make the office more conducive to inspired thinking. This could be as simple as painting the office a new color, having imaginative toys on desks, having a bulletin board filled with creative sayings, or allowing for more personalization of individual workstations.
- *Invest in fun-type training.* Employees at Pixar Animation Studios are sent to ballet courses, encouraged to play a musical instrument, trained to juggle. None of it has a direct bearing on people's ability to do their jobs but it actually makes a huge difference in their ability to bring a creative approach to their work. What could your team do? Take

language classes during a coffee break? Participate in an improvisation class? Learn to draw?

- *Set aside a physical space for creativity.* Fill it with crayons, colored pens, big sheets of paper, and craft supplies. Encourage people to use a percentage of their work time to develop new ideas. Put on some great music to encourage the creative juices! Or provide a sanctuary for people who find that inspiration comes to them in a quiet place. Think of it as an "Intuition-at-Work" room.
- *Discuss what's working.* Many meetings bog down with their focus on problems and challenges. Make sure you devote part of each gathering to a brief discussion celebrating the successes in your office, your company, or on your staff.
- *Discuss what didn't work.* Often, innovative ideas don't work for one reason or another. Mistakes happen! Advertising icon Leo Burnett put it this way: "To swear off making mistakes is very easy. All you have to do is to swear off having ideas." Rather than ignoring that fact, address it.
- *Research what others are doing right.* Is there another team in your company whose members are particularly innovative? Talk to them! If you're a solo entrepreneur, consider talking to others in your field. What do they do that works for them? What are their best practices? Look for ways to brainstorm with other individuals or teams.
- *Create a vehicle for suggestions.* Make it known that new ideas are welcome. Post a question of the week that would help stimulate responses. Put it on a bulletin board, in a suggestion box, or on your company intranet.
- *Be someone who listens.* Creative ideas are often lost when the person in charge doesn't take the time to listen. Make it a priority to listen carefully, elicit opinions, give feedback, and, where appropriate, act on the suggestions.
- *Have fun!* Creative ideas are most easily produced in a lighthearted environment. Start a collection of fun ideas for your company, department, or unit. Ask the staff to suggest ideas for bringing more fun to their work. At least once a

week try out one of the ideas. Injecting some fun into your day-to-day operations can be just the tonic to rejuvenate your staff's creativity.

- *Take frequent breaks.* Encourage people to take short breaks, especially when everyone is working on a tight deadline or some other pressure-producing activity. A shift in routine can reinvigorate thought processes. Do something relaxing or silly—go for a walk, grab a latte, or try to solve a puzzle to relieve the tension.

The word *intuition* comes from the Latin *intueri,* which means "to look within." You have within you and within your team a rich resource. Creative people work from the inside out. They first focus within and look there for their source of wisdom and inspiration. From that wellspring, brilliant new products, ideas, and businesses are manifested and flourish.

gut truster tip

Make it clear to your staff that intuition, creativity, and innovation are important to you and the company. Don't just pay lip service to the idea; back it up with action.

CHAPTER 12

Thrive through Crisis and Chaos

"I respond to fear by listening to my intuition.
One thing I am doing to encourage this within my
workspace is creating a 'chill room' where one
can relax, decompress, do some yoga, meditate,
sit or just be. A quiet oasis where employees
can find peace in the middle of a crazy day."

— CATHLEEN MITCHELL, FOUNDER OF THE COMMUNICATIONS FIRM McROBERTS MITCHELL LLC

We've all experienced it. Despite your best intentions, life be-comes over-the-top stressful. It may have happened after you care-fully planned the presentation to your biggest client. Everything was perfect. But as you're heading to the big meeting you receive a call that your husband was in a car accident and is on the way to the hospital.

Or everything is in place for the promotion of your firm's new product. It's been years in the making, press releases have gone out, the media are interested, your staff is prepped, or-ders are beginning to pour in. And you discover an error in the manufacturing of your product. That's what happened to Steve, the CEO of a major personal care products firm:

We had completed all the prototypes for our product and it worked perfectly. It was a cutting-edge creation. There was nothing out there in the market like it. The first month it was on the shelves we were getting glowing reports from our customers and reviewers. Then, inexplicably, something changed. We began to get a large number of calls to our customer services lines saying our product was defective.

I called the product development team into my office for an emergency meeting. Unfortunately, they were as baffled as I was. They were looking to me for the answer, and, honestly, I felt totally overwhelmed and didn't know where to begin. I talked to my public relations director, and we crafted a message to give to the press who were beginning to catch on to our problem. Frankly, as the day progressed I felt I was becoming more and more ineffective, and I still didn't have a clue as to what the answer was.

Finally, I did what I should have done earlier. I closed the door, asked my assistant to put my calls on hold, sat down, and put my feet up on my desk. I had taken a class on intuition several years prior to this. Since then, my trust in my intuition had gotten stronger and I relied on it more and more, especially when I was in a personal or business crisis. Clearly I needed it today.

I'm a spiritual man, not religious. I know that when I'm overwhelmed I just need to quiet myself and pray. The answers are always there inside of me. They come to me through my intuition. I also know I can crowd them out by being anxious. I've used meditation and dream journaling as tools to help me access this inner wisdom, but I believe the scriptural admonition to "pray without ceasing" is a directive to be mindful that the Resource is always there.

I decided to simply let all the emotions I felt flow over me. The panic, confusion, fear, and anxiety just bubbled to the surface. I tried not to resist anything. When I finally felt that my insides were quiet enough, I posed a simple question: "What is the best course of action for me to take right now?"

I receive much of my intuition visually through images and symbolic pictures. As soon as I asked the question, a short mental slide show began to form inside my mind. First I saw the number 2. Then I saw an image of someone holding two of our products. After that I noticed that the two products looked different. At first I couldn't figure it out.

The three "slides" kept repeating themselves, so I asked a different question: "What's the next step?" This time I didn't see the information. I heard it. It was simply the phrase "talk to Joe." I know a number of Joes, but the one that came immediately to my mind was our contact person at the factory in China where our products are made.

It turns out that my intuition was dead on. I called Joe and learned they had duplicated the mold of our product without informing us. He figured he was doing us a favor in order to keep up with demand. Unfortunately, the specs on the second mold were microscopically off but enough to result in a defective product.

I won't bore you with more details other than to say that after a difficult few months we came out okay, and the product has gone on to become very successful. I thank God for my intuition. Without it, I don't know where we'd be.

Freeze-Frame It

The HeartMath Institute in Boulder Creek, California, has a wonderful technique it calls "Freeze-Framing." I have found it very helpful to use when I'm in situations like those Robert describes above—especially when my anxiety threatens to block out all insightful intuitive messages.

Doc Childre is the founder of the program and author of the book *The HeartMath Solution*. He explains:

When we're internally self-managed–feeling balanced, in control, and powerful–we make our greatest contribution. We act, not react. We think creatively. We communicate clearly. We manage well under pressure. We make good decisions. Our most inspiring leadership qualities emerge. When dozens, hundreds, thousands of employees work in that zone of peak performance, so does the organization.

If you're wondering how to use this information next time you're in a crisis or simply feeling anxious, try the following technique:

1. Recognize the stressful feeling and freeze-frame it. In other words, take time out. For example, see your problem as a still picture, not a movie. Stop the inner conversation you're having about the situation.

2. Make a sincere effort to shift your focus away from your racing mind or disturbed emotions, and concentrate on the area around your heart. Pretend you're breathing through your heart to help focus your energy in this area. Keep your focus there for ten seconds or more.

3. Bring to mind a positive feeling or recall a time in your life when you were having fun. Hold that feeling for a few moments.

4. Now, using your intuition, ask your heart what would be a more efficient response to the situation—one that would minimize stress?

5. Listen to what your heart says in answer to your question. It's an effective way to put your reactive mind and emotions in check. It's like having an in-house source of wise solutions.

You may hear nothing yet feel calmer. You may receive confirmation of something you already know, or you may experience a complete perspective shift, seeing the problem in a more balanced way. Although you may not have control over the event, you do have control over your perception of it and reaction to it.

The techniques taught at HeartMath are more extensive than the simple Freeze-Frame exercise. In fact HeartMath has several software programs and other leading-edge products. Its clinical studies have dramatically demonstrated the critical link between emotion, heart function, and cognitive performance. Its case studies have shown measurable improvements in leadership performance, sales effectiveness, customer service, staff retention, cost reductions, health, and overall performance through the use of its program.

Success in the Face of Crisis

Ken MacDonald is an electrical systems engineer employed by a company that manufactures and sells commercial satellites to companies like DirectTV, XM Satellite Radio, Sirius Satellite Radio, and EchoStar. He's often in situations that require swift solutions in a chaotic and time-sensitive business. He describes a recent intuitive insight this way:

> *While working on the payload configuration of a communications satellite design, our customer suddenly changed the payload requirements, which meant the rewiring of 128 electrical connections. It takes three years to design, build, and test a custom satellite like this, so it's incredibly expensive to make these changes late in the game.*
>
> *After about an hour of working on the problem, I told the project manager (my boss) that I had a solution that required the rewiring of just 16 connections, not 128. But I added that I knew deep inside there was*

another significantly better solution, and though I had no idea what it was, I knew I would find it.

My boss was already pleased with my 16-connection solution and didn't respond to my claim of an even better idea. However, later that day I discovered I could solve the problem by breaking only one wire and inserting a relay in the middle. My new solution was presented to the customer, and he was extremely impressed. What impressed me, though, was the fact that my intuition had told me I had not yet solved a problem that everyone else felt was solved. I had been so certain about this that I told my boss about it before I had a clue as to what it was. I'm known as a problem solver and, as a result, my coworkers think I'm smart. I am smart—because I listen to my intuition and then take action.

How did Ken receive these intuitive impressions that saved his client tens of thousands of dollars?

I believe the key is to simply be aware of what your mind and body are telling you. Sometimes I hear a faint voice, sometimes I just know something, and sometimes my gut tells me which direction to go. These are subtle signals that can easily be missed if you're not listening. Being aware and grounded not only helps me tune into my intuition, it helps me live in the moment and fully experience life.

These stories are not unusual. They represent hundreds more I've heard just like them . . . tales of success in the face of crisis and chaos—stories that have happy endings because their main characters listened to and heeded their intuition.

gut truster tip

When you're in a chaotic situation, make a sincere effort to shift your focus away from your racing mind or disturbed emotions and concentrate on the area around your heart. While keeping your focus there, ask your intuition for a more efficient response to the situation.

CHAPTER 13

What's a Dream Worth?

I've realized that most of my best ideas have followed a good night's sleep.

— THOMAS EDISON, INVENTOR AND BUSINESSMAN

Jean, mentioned in Chapter 6, describes herself as a high school dropout who's now the president and CEO of her $25 million-a-year service business. She credits a dream she had when she was 28 years old as part of what got her started on her path to success. "I was in a grocery store and noticed that there were coins scattered all down the aisles. It stuck me as incredibly odd that everyone was walking right past these gold pieces while I was busy picking them up as fast as I could."

She awoke from the dream with a powerful thought: "I see opportunities where others do not." She describes this dream as helping her understand that she had a divine calling. She felt that she was "wired for business." The dream provided both the catalyst and courage to start her company.

A Source of Ideas, Solutions, and Creative Direction

Jean isn't alone in finding dreams helpful. Successful people in all walks of life have pointed to their dreams as a rich source of ideas, solutions, and creative direction. Pro golfer Jack Nicklaus credits a dream with helping him improve his golf swing after an extended and embarrassing professional slump. The day after his dream, he improved his game by ten strokes.

Former Beatle Paul McCartney woke up from a dream with the tune to the song "Yesterday" running through his mind. "It was just all there," he said. "A complete thing; I couldn't believe it." It rapidly became a pop standard (2,500 versions) covered by everyone from Frank Sinatra to Marianne Faithfull. Thirty plus years later it's still the most played song on the radio.

There are many well-documented tales of creative solutions springing from dreams. German physiologist Otto Leowi credits a dream with enabling him to prove that nerve impulses were chemical rather than electrical. He won the Nobel Prize for this discovery. Rolling Stones guitarist Keith Richards said the riff in "(I Can't Get No) Satisfaction" came to him in his sleep. And the 19th-century chemist Dmitri Mendeleev reportedly dreamed up the periodic table of elements.

In 1845 Elias Howe was trying to invent a practical sewing machine. He was experiencing difficulty with the needle design until a solution came to him in a dream. A tribe of warriors captured him and brought him before their king. The monarch roared, "Elias Howe, I command you on pain of death to finish this machine at once." In his dream the warriors were thrusting their spears toward him in a menacing manner. Suddenly he noticed that at the end of these spears were eye-shaped holes. He awoke from his dream, sprang out of bed, and whittled a needle with an eye in the point. It was a small but incredibly significant change that revolutionized an industry.

Raymond Kurzweil is a pioneer in the fields of optical character recognition (OCR), text-to-speech synthesis, speech recognition technology, and electronic musical keyboards. He's also the author of several books on health and technology. What makes him so productive? He said:

I do all my work while I'm sleeping. Every night before I go to sleep I think about an issue and think about a solution.

In the twilight stage, while I'm dreaming, that''s the most creative time. All the sensors in your head are relaxed. I think about the issue again in the morning and can write a whole chapter of a new book, write a speech, or come up with a new invention in just a few minutes.

A dream is also credited with saving the DuPont Corporation millions of dollars. Their Kevlar vests were in huge demand during the Gulf War and a special high-speed machine was set up to create them. Unfortunately for both DuPont and the soldiers, it kept breaking down. The engineers couldn't figure out what was going wrong until one of them had a dream. He dreamt that he had become part of the machine and saw water spraying around indiscriminately and hoses collapsing. When he awoke he immediately set to work creating some springs that would help keep the hoses open. His dream solution saved the day and probably saved many lives as well.

Sleep on It

Suppose you could go to sleep at night and come up with solutions to your work-related problems? It's really a very cushy job! The requirements? Just a nice soft bed, a little thinking and writing, a pad and pencil on the nightstand. After that you just close your eyes and dream. Upon awakening in the morning, be willing to write down your insights. That's it! Need more detail? Here are some things to do to help you use your sleeping state to help you resolve problems and come up with creative solutions:

- *Keep a dream journal.* This doesn't need to be anything fancy. A notebook or pad of paper beside your bed works great. If you're not concerned with waking your bedmate, a tape recorder could work as well. Before you go to sleep, write a few paragraphs about the decision you're trying to make or the issue you're seeking insight about. You're basically trying to get a data dump from the left side of your brain onto the page.

- *Summarize the issue.* Read the paragraphs you've written and condense them into a one-sentence question. Example: "Should I pursue this new career direction?" Or "How can we speed up the manufacturing process of our widgets?" Others have found it easier to simply ask for information about a concern. "I need information about increasing sales." Or "I would like a dream about a prosperous new direction for my business."

- *Ask the question or state the concern as you drift off to sleep.* Tell yourself that you'll remember a dream that will provide the answer(s) to this question. As you doze off, repeat your phrase softly to yourself, with the mental expectation of receiving an answer. If your mind wanders, gently bring it back to the question.

- *Wake up slowly.* As you wake up try not to come *fully* awake at first. Ask yourself, "Did I have a dream about my concern?" Don't get out of bed. In fact, move as little as possible when you're in the middle of dream recall.

- *Record the dreams or dream fragments.* Even if you don't remember the entire dream, jot down the fragments. Answers in dreams don't always announce themselves in an obvious way. They'll show up through symbolic images, metaphors, feelings, and sensations.

- *Interpret the dream.* There are vast libraries of books on the subject of dream interpretation. However, many tend to reduce everything to a universal symbol. A fire might signify a romantic evening to one person but to you it might be a sign of danger. *You're* the expert on yourself and your dreams.

Here are some items to consider to help you jump-start your interpretation:

- *Look for the solution.* Is there an immediate answer you've received upon awakening? What can you take away from the dream and use in your current situation? Is there any part of your dream that leaps out at you as important and worthy of some further reflection?
- *Identify the symbols.* Are there dream symbols or metaphors that pertain to your question from the night before? How might these be relevant to your question and answer? What pops into your mind when you think about these symbols? Who or what in your life do they remind you of?
- *Describe the dream out loud.* A dream's meaning can become clear when you verbalize it, because we often use plays on words to form pictures. For example, I once had a dream about a pain in my foot. I kept saying, "It hurts to put my foot down." I realized I was unconsciously referring to my inability to "put my foot down" in a situation with a colleague at work. You might also describe your dream in the first person, present tense. This will often evoke some overlooked piece of information.

Without Dreams

What if you're someone who just doesn't remember dreams? Al Eidson, who runs a small PR and marketing company in Kansas City, has a technique for you:

I believe it's important to trust your instincts, but it's difficult to listen to them in the crush of a normal business day. The approach that works best for me is to simply start a project by outlining it in PowerPoint.

This includes pulling the most rudimentary data on the subject, outlining the message points or whatever represents a "start." Doing this the last thing in the day often works best for me. I find that overnight the information will jell into useable and salient knowledge.

The information may not be complete or even completely correct, but the idea will have taken shape, or I'll have a new insight that provides a path. I make enormous progress very quickly.

I think that Edison puts to use what author John Steinbeck has noted: "It is a common experience that a problem difficult at night is resolved in the morning after the committee of sleep has worked on it."

May you and your committee have a good night's sleep!

---

gut truster tip

If you're trying to make a decision, ask for a dream. Ask the question or state the concern as you drift off to sleep. Tell yourself that you'll remember a dream that will provide the answer(s) to this question.

CHAPTER 14

Intuitive Idea Generator

The way to get good ideas is to get lots of ideas and throw the bad ones away.

— LINUS PAULING, WINNER OF NOBEL PRIZES IN BOTH PEACE AND CHEMISTRY

What do you do when you need an idea and you need it fast? Hire a consultant? Delegate? Panic? No to all of those! You have within you a creative genius ready to help you at a moment's notice. You just need a few suggestions to help prime the pump. As master idea generator Albert Einstein said, "In the middle of difficulty lies opportunity." Don't lose hope. Help awaits. Just grab a pen and notebook, roll up your sleeves, complete the exercises below, and, voilà, brilliant answers! You had it in you all the time.

Ask the Right Question

What is the biggest challenge you're facing? Phrase it as a question in at least five different ways. For example:

1. How could we improve employee retention?
2. What would be the best way to improve employee retention?
3. Why the heck can't we keep our good people?
4. Why are people leaving our company in such large numbers?
5. How can we attract employees who want to stay?

You get the idea. After you've generated your list of questions, circle the one that's most compelling. It will be the one that jumps out at you. Remember when you were in school and the teacher asked a question and you knew the answer? It will make you feel like that. Now. . . answer the question and come up with a great solution.

Focus on the Solution

You may not know the exact solution to the problem you're facing. However, there are several ways of focusing on the solution. Ask yourself questions like these: "How will I know the problem has been solved?" "What will I accept as verification?" "How will I feel when my problem is solved?" "How will my life (business, team, etc.) be different when this issue is worked out?" "What will success look like?" If you can begin to focus on the outcome you desire, your intuition will be able to provide you with the most advantageous path to get there.

What Would _____ Do?

Fill in the blank with the name of someone you admire. It can be a former or current boss, your neighbor, your mother or father, a famous historical figure. It doesn't matter whom you choose as long as you view the person as possessing the qualities you need to make this decision. Close your eyes and imagine you are this person. How would he or she approach your issue or problem? Jot down all the ideas that come to you, even if they seem silly, weird, or impossible. Those are usually the best!

Befriend Your Inner Critic

One of the most difficult parts of generating new ideas is that it seems to send your inner critic into high gear. If your inner critic sounds anything like mine, you'll hear such things as: "That's a dumb idea." "That won't work." "Who do you think you are?!" Let me hasten to add that your inner voice (intuition) and your inner critic have nothing in common. Intuitive messages are usually kind and calming and make you feel hopeful and optimistic. The inner critic does the opposite.

Artist and poet William Blake stated, "All great inventions, ideas, businesses and solutions were once simply an idea in someone's mind. What is now proved was once only imagined." In order not to hinder those great ideas, make friends with your inner critic. Tell him or her they have a role in helping you evaluate ideas once you've given them time to develop. Respect your creative process. Let your thoughts percolate for a period of time before you assess them.

Think Like an Alien

If you had just landed on earth from a planet far, far away, you'd constantly be asking who, what, when, where, and especially why. Aliens would have very few preconceived notions, so they'd be open to taking in new information. If you were an alien, what would you want to know about this problem? Quoting Einstein again, "If an idea is not at first absurd, there is no hope for it." Write the questions and answers quickly, along with any ideas that are generated. Don't censor anything.

Write a Quick Q & A

Many people have great success gaining intuitive insight by writing a series of questions about their choices. They'll write, for example:

- If I hire Mary, will the company's sales increase?
- If I hire her, will this be a positive choice?
- Will she communicate effectively with her direct reports?
- Is she a team player?
- What are her strengths?
- What are her weaknesses?

When you've completed your questions, write the answers as soon as they come to you. Don't stop in the middle to analyze your responses.

Repeat the process if you have additional issues to consider. The time to evaluate your answers is after you've finished the intuitive portion of the exercise.

Question Your Assumptions

You may be feeling stuck because you're making incorrect assumptions about a person, idea, or situation. Challenge those notions. Ask yourself questions such as "Is there another way of looking at this?" Or "What might cause someone to act this way?" The obvious can disguise information that may be critical to understanding your situation. Search for ways to look at the situation differently by changing your perspective. How might you view it from the other person's perspective? If you were an outside observer, how would you describe this situation? Be willing to look at your challenge in a number of different ways. When you find yourself thinking "Obviously," question whatever words complete that sentence.

Ask Upside-Down Questions

"The silly question is the first intimation of some totally new development," states British mathematician Alfred North Whitehead. He would probably agree that thinking about your problem from an entirely different, or "upside-down," perspective may provide some innovative solutions. To use this method, jot down a business challenge you're facing. For example, "We want to increase our sale of widgets in Asia." Now come up with rapid-fire answers to the question, "How can we ensure our widgets won't sell in Asia?" Have fun with this! You're looking for outrageous, creative, harebrained, off-the-wall ideas here. When you're done, choose a few of the more intriguing ones and reverse them, that is, write the opposite and evaluate your solutions.

Be Open to New Possibilities

Japanese Zen priest *Shunryu Suzuki* once noted, "In the beginner's mind there are many possibilities; in the expert's mind there are few." Sometimes all it takes to be open to intuitive insight is to have a beginner's mind—curious, interested, willing, and inquisitive.

Listen to music that is outside your comfort zone. Choose a different route to the office. Drive a little slower. Take a train or bus if you usually drive the car. Try a different kind of ethnic food. If you're usually an extrovert, try being quiet and listening. If you consider yourself shy, practice being confident and extroverted. Try writing the answers to some of the exercises on this page with your opposite hand. Do something creative. Learn to knit. Take a foreign language class. Try a new recipe with a food you've never eaten. Find a new hobby. Read a book on an unfamiliar topic. If you're used to reading dense business tomes, try a murder mystery or a romance novel. Have fun! The purpose of all of this is to give your intuitive mind the message, "I am open to new possibilities." It will reward you with rich insight.

Let the Intuitive Muses Provide Answers

Do you ever notice that brilliant answers don't seem to come when you're really focused, intense, and serious? This usually occurs when you need creative insight this very minute. It happens to all of us. You may as well take advantage of this fact and let the muses help you by expanding your options. "Nothing is more dangerous than an idea when it is the only one you have" says philosopher Emile Chartier.

To begin, choose a topic about which you'd like some fresh insight. Write a line or two about it in your notebook. Now take a 15-minute break and do something routine. If you're home—take a shower, wash the dishes, or pet the cat. If you're at the office—take a walk outside, grab a latte, or simply take the elevator down to the lobby. When the 15 minutes are up, grab your notebook again and jot down all the new ideas you have at the moment. The great thing is that the intuitive muses enjoy helping you. You just have to give them a work assignment!

Whenever you're trying to come up with new ideas, keep in mind the wonderful dialog from *Alice in Wonderland*. Alice laughs and says to the Queen, "There's no use trying. One can't believe impossible things."

The Queen replies, "I daresay you haven't had much practice. When I was younger, I always did it for half an hour a day. Why, sometimes I've believed as many as six impossible things before breakfast."

May you believe impossible things and create wonderful possibilities!

gut truster tip

You may be feeling stuck because you're making incorrect assumptions about a person, idea, or situation. Challenge those notions. Ask yourself questions such as "What's another way of looking at this?" Or "What might cause someone to act this way?" The obvious can disguise information that may be critical to understanding your situation.

CHAPTER 15

Liberate Your Inner Innovator

We've put so much faith in analysis and quantification and other areas of left-brain thinking, we've often missed the forest for all the well-examined trees.

— ROBERT EATON, FORMER CHRYSLER CHAIRMAN AND CEO WHO HELPED ORCHESTRATE THE MERGER WITH DAIMLER-BENZ

"Companies that master innovation will inherit the future," states Robert B. Tucker, president of The Innovation Resource and an internationally recognized leader in the field of innovation. His international best seller *Managing the Future: 10 Driving Forces of Change for the New Century* has been translated into 13 languages.

The interest in innovation has exploded over the past several years. Innovation is at the top of the list of many corporate CEOs. The reason? Growth through acquisition has become problematic. It doesn't always deliver the goods. Also, after the merger mania, you have a combined company that simply needs to deliver some organic growth. The only way to do that is through innovation.

Many large companies such as GE and Whirlpool are becoming much more systematic about innovation. It used to be ad hoc or seat of the pants. There were a lot of happy accidents *that created breakthroughs. The fact is, companies don't want to wait for a crisis to create their next breakthrough!*

Innovation has to be a process versus a series of disconnected activities. Some companies say, "Let's improve our new product development process!" What they often fail to understand is that every department in the company needs to be in on generating the ideas. It has to be a comprehensive approach.

Creativity *helps you come up with brilliant ideas.*

Innovation *is the process by which these great ideas are brought to life.*

Intuition *is an overlay of creativity and innovation. It helps you choose which ideas are the winners and which decisions will lead to success. It helps you choose partners and collaborators to partner with (and which not to!)*

All three are vitally important. In 1986 Dr. Denis Waitley and I wrote the book Winning the Innovation Game. *I interviewed 50 leading innovators of the day such as Dr. Jonas Salk, who discovered the polio vaccine; Fred Smith, the founder of Federal Express; Andrew Grove of Intel; and many, many others.*

What really began to emerge from those conversations was that all these innovators were not only responsible for coming up with ideas; they also had to bring them to life. They were all intuition driven. Intuition became part of their decision-making strategy. Intuition would help them discover when a problem existed. It could also answer the question of what would create a positive customer response.

I call it "informed intuition" because many people think of intuition as simply hocus-pocus. In part, it's the result of accumulated experience.

Tucker went on to add a technique that many of the intuitive businesspeople I interviewed mentioned.

When I have to make a decision, I immerse myself in information that is relevant to it. I read trade journals, talk to people, understand the current thinking, and gather data.

Then I use my intuition and truly listen to what my gut is telling me. At a certain point you have to step away from the logical information and begin to tune in to the intuitive. With ever-increasing demands at work, most of us have considerably less time for reflection and thinking. Decisions are made hastily, without considering the alternatives. Innovators avoid this by giving themselves what I call "dream space." It's vitally important.

People often expect that accurate intuition will produce instant success. That isn't always the case as Tucker points out:

There are usually dark days before the innovative products or services take off, before it becomes a hit with the customer. Innovation, by its very nature, means that you're doing something that's never been done before. There are no step-by-step recipes and no market research that can guarantee success. But going with your gut can become a kind of sixth sense that can tell you to "keep the faith and continue" or "throw in the towel."

Intuition doesn't just point you in the direction of success. It will also steer you away from failure. Tucker agrees, adding:

Intuition can help you read people's true intentions and character; it can help you spot trouble spots and think of novel solutions to problems, and alert you very quickly when something's not working. The only time intuition will not work is when we tune it out. When we're greedy or when we're needy, intuition has no ignition. In other words, if I'm desperate or anxious about something, I seem to override my inner knowing.

Why Innovation Is Important

Tucker notes that whether you're part of a large corporation or a "solopreneur," innovation is important. Why? Here are some compelling reasons:

- There have been advancements in technology and you need to keep up.
- Product lifetime is much shorter than it used to be. People replace products much sooner.
- The environment for your service or product has changed.
- Customers are demanding something new, better, more sophisticated or, simply, different.
- Your customers' needs are changing.
- Your competitors have improved their services or products.
- Your customers have stopped buying your services or products.
- Key employees leave.
- Your stock price drops.
- Shareholder returns drop.
- Customers are unable to differentiate your brand from your competitors.

Tap Your Inner Innovator

How can you put this wealth of information to use and tap into your own inner innovator?

- *Be curious!*—Immerse yourself in your topic. Read about it. Talk to others. Do your research. As you're doing this, be aware of what intrigues you, what inspires you to learn more, what compels you forward. Follow that thread. That's your inner innovator leading you in the right direction.
- *Visualize*—What would it look like and feel like if your idea, product, or service were to be successful in the market-

place? Think in both mental as well as emotional images. As you practice this, your intuition will drop clues in your mind about how to most easily achieve your goals.

- *Be different*—Don't do something just because your competitors are doing it. You want to lead the pack. That's what an innovator does! Is there an unusual market you hadn't previously considered?

- *Think differently*—Pretend a psychic has predicted your company (product, service, idea) will be wildly successful this year. Grab a notebook and write out a description of exactly how you'll achieve this success. If you're someone who is more motivated by imminent failure, imagine the reverse! The prediction is that you'll fail miserably this year. Write about what got you there. How could you avoid this catastrophe?

- *Pretend you're the client*—Your biggest customer just called and said she was switching to your competitor. Pretend you can read her mind. What are the reasons she's leaving? What compelling case can you make to get her to stay? What innovations are you willing to make as the result of this insight?

- *Focus on your best/worst decisions*—Think back to a time when you made a particularly successful decision or had such an idea. What did it feel like emotionally? How did it feel in your body? How did you know it was a good decision? Do the same exercise with the worst decision you've made. When you're coming up with innovative ideas, pay attention to how they make you feel. This is your intuitive response system in action.

- *You've won the lottery*—Innovative ideas often get stalled because they're stopped in their tracks by the phrase, "It's not in the budget." Pretend for now that money is no object. Allow the idea factory of your mind to generate unlimited ideas and solutions. After you're finished, go back and create a list of ways to accomplish the most innovative ideas based on your current budget.

- *Business 2.0 readers have voted!*—Your company (idea, product, service) has been voted the most innovative of the year. What are they saying about you? What do you want them to say? What business opportunities would you like this to open up?

- *Honor your fantasies*—(No, not that kind!) If you were to succeed beyond your wildest dreams, what would life look like for you (your team, your company)? Think up some outrageous scenarios. Go for the seemingly impossible! What honors or awards would you receive? Whose recognition would be most important to you? We often limit our ideas of what's possible and therefore drown out the voice of our intuition.

- *Try on a different persona*—Do something different. Take some professional and personal risks. Be courageous! Move out of your proscribed comfort zone. Create a mind's eye picture of yourself as creative, confident, full of ideas, and well liked. Act as if you're that person. What do you feel like? What ideas can this "new you" come up with?

- *Use your imagination* — Many amazing ideas come to those who are willing to be silly or even foolish. In fact, Larry Ellison, CEO of Oracle Corporation, says, "When you innovate, you've got to be prepared for everyone telling you you're nuts." Try this exercise on for size. Imagine that there is such a thing as a wise and business-savvy "Divine Innovator (DI)." Picture him (or her) in any way you want. Perhaps this person has a "magic innovator wand" that allows his or her subjects to come up with great ideas. Close your eyes, focus on the DI, ask him or her a question and allow the responses to pop into your mind.

- *Use metaphors*—Think about the issue or problem you're trying to solve. Now look around your office and choose an object, such as a phone. Ask, "How is the solution to this problem similar to a phone?" Jot down ideas as they come to mind. This allows you to see the connections between seemingly unrelated elements. It allows you to think of the issue differently and thus elicits creative ideas.

- *Tolerate chaos*—Innovative solutions don't usually come in a nice, presentable package. They're wild, paradoxical, and unpredictable. They also don't come when you're applying a logical, rational, or structured approach. Learn to be resilient, patient, and willing to keep trying. If one thing doesn't work, the next one might.

- *Laugh often*—Intuition comes most easily to those who have a lighthearted approach to life. I'll close this chapter with a description of a cartoon I saw recently depicting how Sir Isaac Newton came to form the law of gravity. Four men are sitting separately in a field. Each one is leaning on a trunk underneath an apple tree and all have writing pads in their hands. Three of the apple trees have moderate size apples hanging on their branches, but the fourth has a huge apple hanging just above the head of the man seated beneath its branches. The caption reads, "Anything yet, Newton?"

gut truster tip

Immerse yourself in your topic. Read about it. Talk to others. Do your research. As you're doing this, be aware of what intrigues you, what inspires you to learn more, what compels you forward. Follow that thread. That's your inner innovator leading you in the right direction.

CHAPTER 16

Intuitive Brainstorming

The organizations of the future will increasingly depend on the creativity of their members to survive. Great groups offer a new model in which the leader is an equal among Titans. In a truly creative collaboration, work is pleasure, and the only rules and procedures are those that advance the common cause.

— WARREN BENNIS, FOUNDING CHAIRMAN OF THE LEADERSHIP INSTITUTE AT THE UNIVERSITY OF SOUTHERN CALIFORNIA'S MARSHALL SCHOOL OF BUSINESS

Whether you describe yourself as a "solopreneur," head of a Fortune 500 company, or somewhere in-between, you're constantly challenged by the issue of how to stand out from the competition. This is why business creativity is a necessity, not a luxury. Are you personally open to new ideas and direction? Do you encourage it in your team and team leaders? You should give this serious thought because your career and your business could depend on it.

Why are intuition, creativity, and innovation so important? And what's the difference between them? Here's how it looks to me. Intuition is the hunch, flash of insight, or gut feeling that provides the source for creativity. Creativity springs from intuition, which leads to innovation, which in turn leads to better, more desirable products and services. Obviously, this can translate directly to the bottom line. So how can organizations be structured and managed so that all three are encouraged and fostered? And what can you do to bring imagination and productivity to your work?

Brainstorming is a term coined by advertising executive Alex Osborn in 1941. He believed that conventional business meetings inhibited the creation of new ideas, and his intention was to design a process that would stimulate originality and spark new ideas. According to Osborn, "Brainstorm means using the *brain* to *storm* a creative problem and to do so in commando fashion, each stormer audaciously attacking the same objective." His rules were fairly simple:

- No criticism of ideas
- Go for large quantities of ideas
- Build on each other's ideas
- Encourage wild and exaggerated ideas

Osborn found that when he applied these rules to his meetings, new ideas flourished. His staff was no longer inhibited from putting forth ideas that they felt might be considered "wrong" or "stupid." In fact, he encouraged "silly" thinking because it often resulted in a great new ad campaign.

While the fundamentals of what Osborn considered brainstorming are still with us today, there has been an elaboration of the rules that govern an effective brainstorming session. Following is a description of the basics.

Brainstorming 101

Thomas Carlyle seemed to be describing brainstorming when he wrote, "The lightning spark of thought generated in the solitary mind awakens its likeness in another mind." The dictionary describes brainstorming as "a method of shared problem solving in which all members of a group spontaneously contribute ideas." It's an excellent way of developing a number of creative solutions to a problem. It's efficient, too. Ask a question that requires a creative answer. Then gather a group of people and solicit their input. The intent is for the group to come up with as many radical, silly, funny, and off-the-wall solutions as possible, as rapidly as they can.

Select Your Team

Begin by choosing a note taker to record the ideas on large, poster-size sheets of paper that can be stuck to a bulletin board or along the walls of the room. This will keep all the ideas clearly visible. It's also helpful to use colored pens as an added stimulus to creativity.

The facilitator is the person who writes the statement of intention, gets everything organized, and leads the session itself. If you're the facilitator, your role is to contribute to, but not inhibit, the flow of ideas, and to encourage everyone to participate. Also be prepared with some creativity generators in order to keep the energy crackling and the ideas popping.

Obviously you want to include people familiar with your project, but consider asking staff from different departments to join you. This is a great way to generate some outside-the-box ideas. If appropriate, you could also invite people who are your target audience. If you're trying to come up with ideas for toys, invite kids. If you provide a service to stay-at-home parents, bring them in!

If your group is using brainstorming for the first time, you might send a memo to all participants specifying the time and date along with a brief overview of what to expect. Encourage casual dress. Include the session's focus statement and any additional background information that might be helpful.

Set a Time Limit

There are two schools of thought on the amount of time to set aside for brainstorming. One school says, "No more than 30 minutes!" The other maintains that a good creative session should encompass at least a morning or afternoon in duration. If you choose the longer version, be sure to take frequent breaks to keep minds sharp and creative juices flowing.

Set a Clear Intention

Write a focused, one-sentence question that defines what you want to accomplish. Be specific. If your question is too ambiguous or too general, people won't know where to start. Write this question in big bold words and post it in a place where everyone can see it.

Here are some examples of good brainstorming questions:

- "What events can we sponsor to position our brand as the fashionable walking shoe?"
- "What are some creative ways we could let businesspeople know about personal chef service?"
- "How could we make our furniture line more appealing to the luxury market?"
- "Is there an inexpensive way to communicate that our executive coaching program helps boost corporate creativity?"

Dr. Seuss, the author of many wonderful children's books, provides this challenge that sounds like a perfect way to begin a brainstorming meeting: "Think left and think right and think low and think high. Oh, the thinks you can think up if only you try!"

Suspend Criticism

All ideas, no matter how crazy they may seem, should be encouraged and recorded without comment or criticism from the group. Advertising executive Charles Brower proffered this advice, "A new idea is delicate. It can be killed by a sneer or a yawn; it can be stabbed to death by a quip and worried to death by a frown on the right man's brow."

The brainstorming session itself is *not* the time to evaluate or assess the creative ideas. That comes later. The general goal of brainstorming is to collect as many ideas as possible, making quantity much more important than quality at this initial stage. Philosopher Ludwig Wittgenstein suggests we. . . "[d]o not stay in the barren heights of cleverness but descend into the green valleys of silliness." Your goal is to encourage the production of silly, off-the-wall, ridiculous ideas.

Generate Ideas

Miki Saxon, founder of Ramped Up Solutions, helps companies and entrepreneurs with intuitive brainstorming. She says that "[b]rainstorming helps them spot problems or holes in new products or services; break out of a rut on a subject they know too well; identify a completely new approach to a task or challenge; and find new insights into people and/or situations."

Here are some techniques she uses to inspire creativity:

- Ask questions such as "What would be fun?" "What do you wish you could do?" Or present a statement like "I wish I had a product that did _____." (Fill in the blank.)
- Quit "thinking." You're looking to open up the door to the rest of your brain. Just generate ideas quickly in a stream of consciousness. You want to open a spill gate to let ideas flow.

- Don't create a lot of structure while brainstorming. Structure defeats creative thinking.
- If the group is too large, consider having people work in pairs or threesomes and then report back to the main group.

Ayn Fox, Catalyst of Creativity Lab, trains individuals and companies in the art of creative thinking. She adds the following:

- Ask questions regarding any idea, no matter how crazy, such as "What's tempting?" "What's terrific?" "What's lacking?" Or "How could we change this so it would be terrific?"
- Suggest that individuals in the group doodle a possible solution to the problem. No words are allowed. Fill one-half of the page with images of how they presently perceive the problem, the other half with representations of how it would look if it was solved.
- Encourage the use of metaphors. For example, say your stated intention is to come up with solutions to your production problem. You might choose a random object in the room such as a coffee cup and ask, "How is the production process like a coffee cup?" Or "What else is this problem like?"
- Ask "If you had a magic wand, how would the problem be solved?" or "If money were no object, how would the problem be solved?"
- After the facilitator states a clear intention for the group, put on some type of meditation music. Ask participants to pay attention to any imagery that emerges, no matter how silly, and see if it can connect with the solution.
- Using guided imagery, suggest that each member of the group has a wise "Inner Yoda" that will help them come up with creative solutions for the issue at hand. Ask them to write down whatever imagery shows up; then discuss with them in small groups to see what real possibilities might emerge.

- Pretend you have psychic skills and create future headlines for your industry. Based on trends that you're observing, ask "What will be big news for our industry in 2010?"
- Write a brief article that reflects the headline of the future. Then ask "How did we arrive at this trend?" Brainstorm the answers.

Evaluation Time

Good ideas need to be evaluated, but don't stop the process to discuss any of the ideas until the meeting is completed. Quickly go through the large number of ideas you've generated. Take a thumbs up or thumbs down vote on each of the items. Circle the promising ideas and cross out the others. If there's time and the energy is still high, you might consider looking at each of the selected ideas and seeing if there's a way to improve on them.

Miki Saxon suggests a "gross sort" after a brainstorming session by putting ideas into big piles by subject or concept. Use your intuition to see which idea shines the brightest.

Most of the "good ideas" will need further work, so you'll have to assign someone to develop them. Be sure to specify *who* will do *what* by *when*.

While all of these wonderful ideas may sound like a lot of work, remember to have fun! When you're in that joyful, pleasant, carefree zone, your best ideas, and those of your team, are sure to emerge.

gut truster tip

Find ways to tap into the rich resources of your group's creativity. Don't discard ideas or concepts that at first might seem silly or far-fetched. Those are often the ones that have the seed of brilliance.

CHAPTER 17

Use Your Brain for a Change

Leaders trust their guts.
"Intuition" is one of those good words that have gotten a bad rap.
Intuition is the new physics. It's an Einsteinian, seven-sense,
practical way to make tough decisions. The crazier the times are, the
more important it is for leaders to develop and to trust their intuition.

— TOM PETERS, MANAGEMENT CONSULTANT
AND AUTHOR OF *IN SEARCH OF EXCELLENCE*

Speaking with John Assaraf is like getting a crash course in quantum physics as it applies to business. He has used that knowledge to build four multi-million-dollar companies in the last 19 years. He played a key role in raising over $25 million of private financing to complete a successful IPO on Nasdaq. He built RE/MAX of Indiana, which today generates over $4 billion a year in sales, and in his spare time he wrote the *New York Times* best-seller *The Street Kid's Guide to Having It All.* He's also the founder of the highly successful OneCoach.com Business Mastery program. The list goes on, but you get the idea.

Scientists agree that everything is energy. Intuition is the higher faculty of mind that picks up that energy vibration. This vibration surrounds everything. Think of the last time you walked into a room and you knew something wasn't right. You're picking up on the energy. Intuition is what you know before you think.

My business partner, Murray Smith, is highly, highly, highly left brain. He wants deductive reason to rule! I tell him that there is something that transcends deductive reasoning by a magnitude of a tsunami and that's intuition. He tells me I can use it, but he wants empirical evidence. What he doesn't understand is, with intuition the empirical evidence is that you simply "know."

The shamans, Hawaiian kahunas, and the ancient mystics–they're born to know. They have something we haven't studied a lot in the West. These mystics are trained to look to energy first–what they feel–before they assess what they see, smell, hear, taste, or touch. We don't study this when we get a Harvard MBA!

Feeling is the conscious energy of the vibration that I'm in or picking up on. We have the ability to tap in to the vibration of anything, whether it's a word, person, situation, or business idea. We need to train ourselves to access the higher faculty of mind first before we move to logic and facts. We usually have it backward!

When you use your intuition you're tapping into a sea of energy that offers the biggest library in the world. I see the brain as an electromagnetic switching station. When we alter our brain state from beta to alpha we're much more open to receiving this intuitive information. That's not as mysterious as it sounds. We're in an alpha state when we're daydreaming, meditating, quieting our minds. We may even, in that slightly altered state, be doing everyday things. That's why you get so many great ideas in the shower.

I asked John to explain how he and Murray work out their differences given their widely divergent styles of decision making. He gave me an example:

I had a strong intuition several months ago that we should offer a Mastermind group option to our OneCoach.com members. He was strongly opposed to it, claiming it would be a lot of work, take too much time, and be difficult for a number of other reasons.

I just had a feeling this would work. We have an agreement that if something is my area of responsibility, I make the call. And vice versa. The results? I wrote the sales letter to our membership, and a week later we had made $500,000 off of that one letter. Our members loved the idea.

What happens when he needs to accept the outcome of Murray's more logical, left-brained process? He says with a laugh:

That's easy! I use my intuition and usually decide to trust his deductive reasoning. We may come at a solution from a very different method. However, the bottom line is that I like him and trust him. We both have similar objectives—we want to enjoy life, make a contribution to the world, create abundance, and assist others to do the same. We just have a very dissimilar path to getting us there. And . . . I hasten to add I think my way is much easier!

The Non-local Mind

In reality, scientists have yet to find anything in the body that defines either intuition or, more generally, consciousness. Where does "the mind" as we know it exist? As David Chalmers, a philosopher at the University of California at Santa Cruz said in a *Scientific American* article, "It's time to bite the bullet and admit that consciousness is another force altogether, on a par with matter and energy."

Dr. Larry Dossey is an author and internist who lectures widely on the topics of spirituality and science. He suggests there is an aspect of our mind that defies space and time limitations.

He uses the term *non-local* mind, a concept coined and used in contemporary quantum physics.

He writes in his book *Recovering the Soul:*

> *The non-local model is not confined in space and time to the brain and body, although it may work through the brain and body. And it is not confined to the present moment. Infinite, and by inference immortal, eternal, omnipresent—all of these are consequences of anything that is non-local, not just mind. As a result, if mind is non-local, there is one mind, or Universal Mind, which . . . the West has regarded as the Soul.*

This opens up interesting questions about intuition. My position in this book is that intuition comes from two general sources. The first is a quick processing of subconscious information. You might use this when you're making a hiring decision and you observe the applicant's style of clothes, manner of speaking, and body language and come up with an instinctual impression of the applicant. The second type of intuition is what Dossey and Assaraf are alluding to above. We have access to a larger, more infinite pool of knowledge through the "non-local" mind, and we connect to it through our intuitive knowing.

Bell's Theorem is named for its author, Irish physicist John Stewart Bell. He demonstrated mathematically that the speed at which information can travel from point A to point B is not, as Albert Einstein's Special Theory of Relativity stated, limited to the speed of light or less. Dr Nick Herbert, also a physicist and author of the book *Quantum Reality,* maintains that when A connects to B nonlocally, nothing crosses the intervening space, and that no matter how far A is from B, the connection is instantaneous.

How does all this relate to intuition? You have a connection to an amazing wealth of information at your disposal through your extended consciousness. When you're thinking about how your factory is doing in Singapore or wondering how to make a sales pitch to your client in Boston, you can pick up information instantly. You don't need to be there in person observing what's going on. It also explains my work as an intuitive and my seemingly implausible ability to tell you, with no rational way of knowing, what will motivate a decision maker to choose your company over the competition.

Interestingly, this information about the nonlocal mind is not new. It's reminiscent of what the philosopher Patanjali wrote in the second century BCE:

> *When you are inspired by some great purpose, some extraordinary project, all your thoughts break their bonds. Your mind transcends limitations, your consciousness expands in every direction, and you find yourself in a new, great and wonderful world. Dormant forces, faculties, and talents become alive, and you discover yourself to be a greater person by far than you ever dreamed yourself to be.*

Outside the Box

Let's bring this lofty discussion back to earth. Organizational psychologist Ian Percy believes that intuitive thinking is one of the ways we access the greater wisdom that the nonlocal mind taps into. Ian works with senior executive teams, helping them transform their organizations by changing how they think. In a recent speech entitled "Thinking Without a Box," he notes that many organizations reach what he calls a "perilous plateau" where creativity, new thinking, and innovation are stalled.

"You can't get off the plateau with cost containment initiatives or mergers and acquisitions, bringing in new people, remodeling, or even restructuring. You can only do it by changing how you think." He asked the audience to stand and open their arms in front of them.

Imagine that space between your arms as representing your agreement with the world. It's filled with your perspectives, assumptions, actions, perceptions, and beliefs.

Within that field represented by the boundaries of your arms are the options that you see. We spend 90% of the time within those boundaries. However, existing outside of those boundaries is a living thing. I call it "All That Is Possible." Each of us receives faint signals from that other place. However, most of us try to fight it off. The information doesn't seem to fit with our preconceived notions. A precious few tap into it and go on to have extraordinary success in both their business and personal lives.

For most of us, our minds are set in frames, and sometimes we lose out on incredible opportunities because they don't "fit" the frame! Imagine someone comes to you with a great business idea. If that opportunity is represented by a 10" x 6" frame and your mind will only allow a 9" x 5" frame, that opportunity will go elsewhere. Intuition is the part of your mind that recognizes the knock on the door and alerts you to the fact a change in thinking is required in order to easily accept this opportunity.

If all of this talk about nonlocality, quantum physics, and energy vibration seems a bit heavy, perhaps a quote from Lewis Carroll's classic, *Alice in Wonderland,* might lighten things up. "Dear dear! How queer everything is today! And yesterday things went on just as usual. I wonder if I've been changed in the night. Let me think: was I the same when I got up this morning? I almost remember feeling a little different."

gut truster tip

When you use your intuition, you're tapping into a sea of energy that offers the biggest library in the world. A consistent practice of meditation or simply quieting the mind will help you access this vast wealth of information.

CHAPTER 18

How to Blink

*I believe that the task of making sense of ourselves and our
behavior requires that we acknowledge there can be as much
value in the blink of an eye as in months of rational analysis.*

— **MALCOLM GLADWELL, AUTHOR OF *BLINK* AND *THE TIPPING POINT***

Malcolm Gladwell's best-selling book *Blink: The Power of
Thinking Without Thinking* has popularized a form of intuition
Gladwell calls "thin-slicing." He speculates that we can make
highly accurate decisions with very limited amounts of information. "Thin-slicing refers to the ability of our subconscious to find
patterns in situations and people based on very narrow slices of
experience," he explains.

Deciding to accept a new job is one of the more significant decisions you may have to make. Most of us do our research by talking to colleagues about the position, making inquiries, going on
interviews, reading background about the company, and so on.
It's the way you're supposed to do it, right?

However, if you're really honest with yourself, you probably
had a gut feeling about the position right from the start. It might

have been when you walked into the room for an interview or the way you felt when you drove your car into the company parking lot. Perhaps it came even sooner—when you first heard about the job. Instead of trusting that instant when you knew in your gut the position was right for you (or not), you probably proceeded to do your homework and gather information. After all, is it really possible to accurately know something in the blink of an eye?

Gladwell posits that we understand a great deal without necessarily being able to explain why and how. We can frequently make some of our best decisions in mere seconds. We think without thinking. While he doesn't use the word *intuition* in his book, he describes a form of it that is predicated on sizing up situations and determining how we feel about a person or situation based not on new information but rather on our accumulated experiences.

Snap Judgments

What exactly are you responding to when you interview for the new position and have a strong gut feeling that the job isn't right for you? Your spouse is telling you to take the offer. Your research hasn't turned up anything untoward. The job description matches your skills and your goals for a new position. What to do? Pay attention! You are picking up on an indication that something is amiss. You ignore the symptoms of your unease at your peril.

It's difficult to accept these snap judgments. You're perceiving something that your reasoning mind can't make sense of. Gladwell comments:

I think we are innately suspicious of this kind of rapid cognition. We live in a world that assumes that the quality of a decision is directly related to the time and effort that went into making it.

Thin-slicing is not an exotic gift. It is a central part of what it means to be human. We thin-slice whenever we meet a new person or have to make sense of something quickly, or encounter a novel situation. We thin-slice because we have to, and we come to rely on that ability because we are good at it.

Gladwell isn't saying that all snap judgments are good ones. He believes that when they're backed by experience, training, and knowledge, we can learn to make excellent decisions quickly and accurately—in the blink of an eye.

Nonlinear Thinking

Doctor Maurice Ramirez describes himself as someone who believes in Gladwell's theories. He teaches people to recognize patterns via "non-linear thinking," which is how he explains intuition. When he arrived as an emergency consultant in storm-ravaged New Orleans, he found a number of medical personnel, also recently arrived, who were unfamiliar with hurricanes and their physical effects on human beings.

Before their arrival they had been told in detail what the hurricane had done and what to expect in the way of injuries. This is a process Doctor Ramirez calls *pre-framing*. As a result, the emergency teams responded to what they had been led to anticipate rather than to actual conditions. Ramirez told the teams they needed to intuitively trust in what they already knew—namely, that certain injuries require a particular response, no matter what it was that caused the trauma. Once they got out of "thinking" mode and into responding instinctively based on their years of experience, better outcomes for victims quickly became the norm.

Lance Powell is an engineer who specializes in large turbine-powered generators. He's often called upon to join a SWAT team whose mission is to track down and eliminate equipment problems. The rational and logical approach usually rules with this group. However, he has become a wary convert to the intuitive approach:

Several years ago, one such mission took us to the edge of the North Sea in England and right into the middle of a fascinating puzzle where our collective gut instinct provided the only solution.

It seems that a recently rebuilt turbine was showing an unexplainable increase of temperature in the first of several internal stages. The customer was happy with the power output, but because there was an abnormal temperature reading, the unit would have to be thoroughly checked in order to satisfy safety requirements.

The best way to perform this check would have been to shut the entire unit down so we could get inside for a thorough examination. But the "patient" weighed 20 tons and was running at 1,000°F, which meant it would take three days to cool down enough to allow us to begin work. Add another nine days of outage to do the investigation, and it could have cost the customer $10 to $20 million during what was then a time of peak demand. So we had to come up with another way.

I felt instinctively that there wasn't any significant issue with this turbine. Nonetheless, we began a labor-intensive process of gathering external data. And as we did, the team began to speculate. Were the first-stage turbine blades designed backward? Or worse, installed backward? Either of these could have caused the problem. We individually and collectively came to the conclusion that there was nothing inherently or dangerously wrong with the unit. Though we didn't really know what was actually going on inside that monster, we just knew—really knew—that those blades were not installed backward and that the unit was safe.

Because my fellow team members had similar feelings—something engineers don't readily confess to—I wrote into my report that despite the popular hypothesis, we were confident that (not "we felt" that) the blades were fine and the unit would continue to generate power without generating problems.

This explanation quickly gained traction with our management, who were able to live with an incorrect blade installation but would have a difficult time with an embarrassing inability to logically and rationally diagnose a problem.

The result was a grudging acceptance by management and a change in insurance that made our company liable for any damages caused by "backward-blades" over the next four years. That's how it was left as we left jolly old England.

Three and a half years later, probably during a period of low power demand, the customer decided to open up the unit and check it out. Their chief engineer, who had discreetly admired our "guts" in declaring the unit okay, called late in the afternoon to let us know the blades had, in fact, been installed correctly.

Naturally, we were enormously curious about what might have caused the temperature aberration, so after high-fives all around, we began an animated half-way-around-the-world coinvestigation. The unit was to be open for just a few hours, so we feverishly gathered data long into the night.

Bottom line: We found nothing. But most important, we found nothing wrong! So in the end, the issue was unresolved, but our collective gut feeling was verified.

Later, after looking closely at all the data we'd gathered, we concluded the errant indication was most likely caused by an unusual flow pattern around the temperature sensor, resulting in a localized heating of a small pocket of steam. This was so minor that it couldn't have realistically been called a problem, which meant the combined intuition of my team had saved an important customer tens of millions of dollars.

Several years have passed since then, and the unit is still running. I feel compelled to add that to this day it's running flawlessly.

How to Thin-slice

How can you learn and utilize the process of thin-slicing? It's all about intuition! The following three questions will help you access the mental state required to make use of this important skill.

1. *"What's my first impression?"* Train yourself to ask this question before beginning the process of analysis and research. Note your response and store it away for future reference. The answer you receive shouldn't preclude doing your homework on the subject at hand. However, when you use your intuition first and hone your skill through repetition, you'll find you have quick, ready, and accurate insight at your disposal whenever you need it.

2. *"What do I need to know?"* Asking this question alerts you to additional information. It gives you insight into what may be just outside your level of conscious awareness. What's wrong (or right) with the situation you're observing? It's helpful to stay emotionally neutral or open when you ask this question. What insight comes to you naturally? Simply observe it. Don't judge it.

3. *"What's the best course of action?"* What pops into your mind when you ask this question? There's a big difference between using your intuition and impulsive, irresponsible decision making. You need to use both sides of your brain. Your intuition will provide quick and ready insight and the logical, rational side of your brain will provide the information about how to most effectively and responsibly execute your plan of action. Again, it takes practice. If you were just beginning to learn to play a piano, you wouldn't expect yourself to be a concert pianist within the first week. So it is with intuition. You learn by a series of small steps. How do you experience an intuitive yes response? How does an intuitively conveyed "Don't go in that direction" feel to you? The answers present themselves in quick flashes, a sudden insight, an unexpected feeling, or a certain knowing. Only

you have the key to unlock how it communicates in your own body, mind, and spirit. Once you find that key, you'll find success.

gut truster tip

"What's my first impression?" Train yourself to ask this question before beginning the process of analysis and research.

CHAPTER 19

Profile of an Intuitive Sales Pro

A sale is not something you pursue; it's what happens to you while you are immersed in serving your customer.

— ANONYMOUS

Imagine for a moment having a reliable source of information available any time you need it that can tip you off to a prospect's primary buying motivator. Do they want service? No problem. Are they looking for quality? Coming right up. Do they simply want to make a lot of money? You got it.

You don't have to imagine such a scenario. With a little practice, you can become adept at determining how to focus your sales presentation and how best to approach your prospect. Should you be laid back or enthusiastic? Factual or emotional? When you know how to use your intuition, you'll know what it takes to close the sale.

Intuition is the secret weapon of many successful sales leaders. Ask them about it, though, and they're likely to describe it as "gut instinct." Sound familiar? Of course it does, because whether you admit it or not, you're highly likely to have experienced it yourself and just as likely to have ignored its messages.

The Intuitive Salesperson

The fact is, every salesperson receives intuitive information about how to approach and effectively work with his or her clients and customers. It's both a gift and a skill, and the more you practice it, the better you get at it. Roy Rowan, author of a study on intuition, said, "This feeling, this little whisper from deep inside your brain, may contain far more information—both facts and impressions—than you're likely to obtain from hours of analyzing data." How do you know when you're tapping into this rich resource? Following is a profile of folks who use it effectively.

Intuitive salespeople

- see alternatives and possibilities rather than hard and fast rules;
- sense what's going on in the heart and mind of their client and apply the most effective approach;
- are able to deal with ambiguous issues;
- stay focused and neutral in chaotic situations;
- are adept at reading concealed or unspoken information and raising it to the level of open dialog;
- produce win-win solutions to difficult challenges;
- are able to solve complex problems where data is often incomplete;
- are practiced at creating a sense of high motivation for themselves and others;
- foresee problems and set about solving them before a crisis emerges;
- are adaptable to a wide variety of cultures, diversity, and belief systems;
- focus on similarities and connections, not differences; and
- listen deeply to others' needs, wants, and desires.

After looking at the list, you'll probably feel even more inspired to learn how to use and expand the valuable inner resource of your intuition to succeed in sales. Here are some tips from the intuitive sales pros I interviewed.

Keep Your "Inner SalesPerson" Positive

Pay attention to what you tell yourself about your sales prospects and your life. If your "self-talk" is positive and optimistic, your personal and business life will reflect that. Try a simple experiment. Close your eyes and say the following to yourself for about 30 seconds: "I'll never get ahead. I'm not good at sales. I won't make my quota this month." How do you feel? Depressed? Demoralized? Hopeless?

Now do the same experiment and focus on these statements: "Things have a way of working out." "I'm learning some new skills and things are beginning to change for me." "Today I'll take steps that will open up opportunities for more income." "I have a great product and I enjoy letting people know about it." Now how do you feel? Hopeful? Optimistic? More confident? When you're in this state, it's much easier for you to be open to intuitive messages pointing you to avenues of increased prosperity.

Use the Power of Silence

As any good salesperson will tell you, "Sometimes the best thing to do is 'shut up.'" But there are times when you also need to silence your mind to receive valuable intuitive insight. When you need help making a decision—pause, take a deep breath, reflect on the question, and allow the intuitive impressions to come to you. Intuition is often described as "still and quiet." It doesn't shout out the answer. It is much subtler. You may, in fact, feel as though you're making up the answer. The truth about the wisdom you receive will only be known when you act on the information.

If your workplace doesn't lend itself to quiet reflection, get out of the office and take a walk or take a seat in your car.

Pay Attention to Your Energy

If a sales strategy or decision leaves you feeling drained or bored, that's a clear message from your inner guidance saying, "This won't work," or "Try something new and different." Conversely, if you feel energized and enthusiastic, your intuition is giving you the green light to continue with your plan of action.

Build Some Downtime into Your Daily Schedule

It might make logical sense to pack sales calls into every moment in order to make efficient use of your workday but not for the intuitive sales pros. They value having a breathing space. They use it for reflection, daydreaming, and thinking. One person said, "I've lost more sales when I'm overwhelmed and stressed. When I build some downtime into my schedule, I'm relaxed and things happen effortlessly. I catch people at just the right time. Opportunities come my way without me chasing after them. It's like I'm a sales magnet when I'm in the flow!"

Envision Your Success

Spend time each day imagining your ideal work life. What does success look like? What does it feel like? Imagine you are living it now. What are you wearing? What are you feeling? Who are the people around you? We are often quite clear about what we *don't* want. The path to success comes from spending time thinking about what you *do* want. What does an ideal day, month, or year look like to you? Being clear about what you want is often the first step in being able to create it. Successful people visualize their goals and dreams. Your intuition can help you achieve success when you know what you want to achieve.

Pay Attention to the Message You're Sending

John Assaraf, mentioned previously in Chapter 17, has built four multi-million-dollar businesses and now mentors entrepreneurs through his company, OneCoach. In his sales trainings, he advises students to watch their inner dialog. "If your thoughts are on 'I have to make this sale in order to pay my mortgage or make my car payment,' your energy is in the wrong place. Your client will pick up on it immediately." Instead, he recommends students stay focused on the qualities of kindness, honesty, caring, authenticity, and doing the right thing for the individual. You want the client to feel good about you and about doing business with you. This attitude may not result in an immediate sale, but it pays off in the long run."

Create a Definition of Your Perfect Customer

Let's face it; it's no fun working with people you don't like. You probably spend a lot of time with your clients. No one looks forward to hanging out with people who are cranky, difficult, and demanding. Turn the tables! Identify the qualities of those you've most enjoyed working with, currently or in the past, and begin to magnetize more of the same.

Stacey Hall and Jan Brognicz are experts on this topic and the authors of *Attracting Perfect Customers*. They suggest you stop *looking* for your perfect customers and *attract* them instead. Sound too good to be true? They believe a "perfect customer" list is an important part of the strategy to easily and effortlessly attract those clients.

How would you describe them? Do they have a good sense of humor? Perhaps they simply pay their bills on time. You may enjoy working with them because they appreciate you and your hard work. Possibly you like them because you and they have similar values. Whatever your reasons, create a written list of the attributes and characteristics of that perfect customer.

This list will "prime the pump" of your intuitive mind, so next time you're on a sales call, remember your list. Ask your intuition, "Does this person or company match my perfect customer profile?" If you feel excited, pleased, and energized by the thought of working with this customer, pay attention! Your intuition has just served up an affirmative answer!

Take the Time and Make the Sale

Be sure to set aside time to routinely check in with your intuition. It won't be long before you'll be experiencing faster, stronger, and more accurate insights. Though intuition can be described as a secret weapon, there's no big secret about how to use it. Follow the suggestions I've outlined above and the more specific techniques in the next chapter and begin to reap the rewards of this powerful competitive advantage.

gut truster tip

Keep your "inner salesperson" positive. Try language that makes you feel hopeful and positive. Intuitive information will present itself more easily if you're open and receptive.

CHAPTER 20

The Power of
Intuitive Selling

*People with high levels of personal mastery do not set out to
integrate reason and intuition. Rather, they achieve it naturally—as a
by-product of their commitment to use all the resources at their disposal.
They cannot afford to choose between reason and intuition, or head and heart,
any more than they would choose to walk on one leg or see with one eye.*

— PETER SENGE, AUTHOR OF *THE FIFTH DISCIPLINE*

Before you begin selling your product or service to a prospect, you'll want to get as much factual information as possible. You'll need to do your research. However, this data may not tell you what the client really needs or how to most effectively work with the individual or team. This is where intuition becomes your most valuable research tool.

Successfully making the sale requires that you process hundreds of pieces of information subconsciously. You must develop and trust your ability to use your intuition to read between the lines. Do you press a client for the sale, or do you back off and wait? Are clients motivated by the lowest price you can offer or is the quality of your product or service the prime impetus for buying

from you? Many times, logic and analysis will provide that information. On other occasions, your gut feelings or instincts—your
intuition—will be the resource you look to for those answers.

Intuitively Creating Value for the Customer

Richard Whiteley is the principal of the Whiteley Group, an
international speaking and consulting firm. He cofounded the
Forum Corporation and helped build it into a 700-person training and consulting company. Intuition has been an important factor in his success, and he shares this knowledge when he speaks
on the topic of *Selling Through Service:*

> *Using intuition helps a salesperson get off her own agenda. In sales you're
> trained to have a call plan. You're instructed to figure out what you're going
> to say and what you want your prospect to do as the result of your plan. Then
> you run in and follow your plan.*
>
> *Of course it's important, but having a plan alone will not get you the order.
> You need to understand your buyer's needs, and that's where intuition is
> invaluable. However, it's difficult to use it if you're myopically following your
> plan and the goal of closing the deal. The job of the salesperson is to create
> value in the moment with whomever he or she is with, whether that person is
> buying or not. If you're there creating value, you have to be paying attention
> to the person.*
>
> *I tell people to become adept at "full body listening." You're not just listening
> to the words. You're listening to energy, language, and subtle clues that give
> you information about what your prospect really needs. Listening like that will
> bring powerful intuition into the plan and result in a happy client, increased
> profitability, and ease in the sales process.*

Mark Murray has participated in one of Whiteley's training
programs. He credits the information with helping him become a
national sales leader in his industry. When I asked him how he ex-

plains his success, he told me that before he meets with a client he would close his eyes and quiet his thoughts. Then with pen in hand, he would ask his intuition, "What do I need to know about this company or this individual?" He'd jot down all images, feelings, and words as rapidly as they came to him. The answers come to him as he writes. Mark's competition simply scratches their heads in wonder over his results.

Several of the intuitive salespeople I interviewed had a technique similar to Mark's. They might ask questions in their mind before approaching the prospect or use a more structured method such as closing the door, shutting their eyes, and formally asking their intuition for insight about how best to connect with their customer.

Before Your Next Sales Call

A number of the sales pros said they used a variation on the following exercise before ever meeting or talking with a client. There often wasn't an opportunity to read body language, hear someone's voice, and, in some cases, have any conscious knowledge about this person at all beyond perhaps knowing a name. Somehow the pros were able to garner significant insight into the prospect without this information. While this may sound as though it's stretching the boundaries of intuition into the psychic realm, try it anyway. If done with an open mind and a little practice, you may find it results in happier clients, increased sales, and ease of negotiation.

Before you call on your next client, set aside at least 15 uninterrupted minutes. Feel free to change the wording or to add your own questions to those below. Write quickly. Don't *think* about the answers.

You may know by now the primary means by which your intuition communicates with you. However, for the purpose of this exercise pay attention to *all* of the responses that you receive to each question. For example, in response to question 4—"What's the biggest problem they're facing?"—you might receive an *image* of customers walking out the door empty-handed. (That doesn't need much interpretation!)

The answer you receive to question 5—"What are the consequences of not acting on this problem?"—could be *knowing* that the company is in serious trouble.

The *words* "We can increase customer retention" may come to you in response to question 7—"How can I (my product or service) help them with this concern?"

Also be aware of any *physical sensations*. You might ask question 10—"Do I want to work with this client?"—and your gut feeling may indicate the answer is no.

Let's begin. Intuitive insight comes most easily when you've closed your eyes, taken some slow relaxing breaths, and centered yourself. Bring the client or company into your mind's eye and focus on them for a few moments.

You may not receive information about every question. If not, skip to the next question. You can come back to it later. If doing an exercise like this is new to you, you may feel as if you're making it up. That's okay, too. The proof is in the results. Simply notice and write down everything you're feeling, sensing, hearing, or seeing in a journal. Stay open and allow the information to flow without judgment. The time to evaluate the responses will come later.

1. Name of company
2. Name of prospective client
3. What do I need to know about this client?
4. What's the biggest problem the client is facing?
5. What are the consequences of not solving this problem?
6. How can I (my product or service) help with this concern?
7. What opportunities is the client trying to create?
8. What is the best way to approach this prospect?
9. How can I be most helpful to him or her beyond the product or service I offer?
10. Do I want to work with this client? If not, why not?

11. Is there anything about the team (company, department) I should be aware of?
12. What should I know about my competition?
13. What can I do to win this account?

Evaluate Your Answers

What do your intuitive responses indicate? Do you now have enough information to allow you to proceed with confidence? It's helpful to keep a notebook specifically for this exercise. The only way to gain confidence is to put into practice the information you've received.

After you've made your sales call, pull out your journal and look at the information you wrote. Use this opportunity to evaluate the intuitive information you had received. Where were you "spot on?" What worked? What didn't work? Were you able to be "present," listening for intuitive insight when you were on the call? Or were you more focused on your sales spiel and forgot to check in?

Was there information you received that doesn't appear to be quite accurate or was outright wrong? That's fine, too. You're practicing developing your intuition. You'll use this information to refine what works and what doesn't. It's not unlike learning to drive a car or to play racquetball. The more you do it, the better you get at it, until it simply becomes second nature.

Of course this exercise is not meant to replace the normal due diligence required before making a sales call. You'll still want to read the company's annual report, check out its Web site, and read what the media have to say about the company. It's just that now you'll have an additional and much more powerful level of information at your disposal.

You'll notice that much of the focus of the questions in the above exercise is about the buyer and the buyer's needs. Asking "what's in the sale for me?" won't elicit the response you need to win the account. Legendary speaker and salesman Zig Ziglar states it so eloquently when he says, "You can get anything in life that you want, if you'll help enough other people get what they want."

Jill Konrath is the chief sales officer of Selling to Big Companies. She helps salespeople get their foot in the door and win big contracts in the corporate market. She emphasizes how important it is to "use your brain and think for your prospective and existing customers."

Jill adds: "They're so busy putting out fires, they lack time for problem solving, strategic thinking, creative alternatives, or even reflection. A seller who consistently brings business ideas to the relationship becomes indispensable—winning contracts with minimal competition and at full dollar value."

Intuition helps you understand your customer and provide the creative strategies and insight that Jill alludes to. It's the inner voice that says, "Try this." "Here's the information you need." Or "Check this out." Listen to that voice. It's what successful people do.

gut truster tip

Before your next sales call, close your eyes, take a slow, deep breath, and ask two questions: (1) "What's the biggest problem this client is facing?" (Pause.) (2) "How can my product (service) help the client solve this problem?" Tune in via your intuition and listen for the answer.

CHAPTER 21

I Knew That Would Happen!

It's imperative to listen to your intuition because you can head a
blossoming crisis off at the pass. You have to figure out how intuitive
impulses feel to you and allow it to become your partner in your success.
It will never lead you astray.

— ROBERT TUCKER, BUSINESS INNOVATION EXPERT AND AUTHOR OF *MANAGING THE FUTURE*

One of the questions I'm frequently asked is, "If you're so intuitive, why haven't you ever won the lottery?" The answer is "I did" (sort of). A few months after I was married to my husband, Gary, I woke up early one Wednesday morning with six numbers running through my head. I found I could neither fall back to sleep nor stop the numbers from endlessly repeating themselves in my mind.

I had never played a lottery before, but it occurred to me that these numbers might represent a lottery win. Gary was snoring beside me; I shook him gently and said, "How many numbers are in the Massachusetts State Lottery?"

"Six," came his mumbled response.

"I think I might have the winning lottery numbers," I replied.

He was on his feet, grabbed a paper and pen, and was ready to write down the numbers before I barely had the previous words out of my mouth. I've never seen him wake up that fast since!

With the "winning numbers" in hand, Gary agreed to play them in the Wednesday lottery. I promptly put the whole thing out of my mind until Friday morning when I casually asked over breakfast if he'd checked on whether our numbers had won.

He confessed that he'd had a crisis at work and had forgotten to play the game on Wednesday but hastened to add that he had placed bets for both Thursday and Friday.

We took out the newspaper to find the lottery list. You guessed it . . . My numbers were the winning numbers for $5.2 million on Wednesday—the day I received the information and the day he *didn't* play it.

Sigh . . . So close and yet so far away. But, yes, I'm still married to him.

Should Have Trusted Her Gut

Patricia Aburdene is an advocate of corporate transformation and author of *Megatrends 2010*. She had a similar unfortunate experience with finances.

I had grown my investments to $2 million thanks to some Internet stocks, two of which had made a $100,000 profit.

Each evening I would look over my portfolio online and enjoy the fact that I had been able to create this abundance. I would also pay attention to any intuitive hits I might get from perusing the stock listings. I was casually doing this one night after dinner when my attention was drawn to the stocks Exodus and Inktomi, the very ones I'd made the largest profit on. I heard an inner voice state, "Watch those stocks. Get ready to sell!" It was crystal clear.

Wouldn't you know, the stocks soon began a downward trend after months of steady upward growth? Unfortunately, I became paralyzed with fear. What if

my intuition is wrong? I knew I should take at least some of the money out.
But I kept thinking that the stock should go up and used my logical mind to
completely override the intuitive message I had received. I ended up losing both
$100,000 profits by riding them down to nothing. It was an important and
expensive lesson to learn. From then on, I learned to heed those inner
messages."

If you're honest with yourself, you've done it too. It's those times you said, "I should have trusted my gut. I knew something was wrong with ____ and I went ahead anyway." Maybe you didn't do it as dramatically as Patricia and I did, but it's important to pay attention to those lapses because they can teach you just as much as the times that you trusted your intuition and things worked out. Let's take a walk down memory lane and see if we can jog some of those recollections.

1. Name someone you shouldn't have trusted but did anyway. What were the signs? How did you know?
2. Describe a time you listened to someone else's advice and ignored your own inner wisdom.
3. When did you have a strong inner message to walk away from something and headed toward it instead?
4. When did you "just know" something but allowed logic or reason to steer you in the wrong direction?
5. Have you ever said, "I just knew that would happen!" What did you know and how did you know it?
6. Have you ever hired someone because his references checked out even though you had a strong feeling he wasn't right for the job? What do you wish you had done differently?
7. Describe a time when you knew you were off track either personally or professionally. What were the indications of this and what do you wish you'd done differently?

8. Your boss (company, partner) was going in a direction you knew wouldn't work. What did you say? What could you have said or done differently?
9. The analysis and research all pointed in one direction. You knew in your gut that success lay in the opposite route. How do you wish you had responded?
10. You chose a job that you knew you shouldn't take. How did you know that and what happened?

Did Trust Her Gut

Just so I don't leave you on a low note, I'd like to include a story from BJ Gallagher, a consultant, speaker, and author of *Women's Work Is Never Done*. It illustrates one of those occasions when it's all too easy to override a gut feeling and simply go with logic.

Jeff and I were scheduled to go to Hawaii in early summer to conduct a workshop at a professional conference. We had known each other for years, as we were both management consultants, but we had never had the opportunity to work together before. Jeff had called me months earlier, asking if I was interested in getting on the program for this conference. My mouth said yes but something in my body said no.

As the months rolled by, that "no" feeling got stronger. I kept trying to ignore it as I'd made a commitment to Jeff, and our proposal was accepted by the conference organizers. But the feeling just wouldn't go away.

Finally, the "no" I was feeling became so insistent that I had to pay attention. I called Jeff.

"Jeff, this is going to sound totally crazy, but I can't go to the conference next month. I don't even have a logical reason why . . . all I know is that my intuition is telling me not to go. The feeling gets stronger the closer we get to the conference–it's like every cell in my body is screaming in unison, 'Don't go! You're not supposed to be there.' So I feel bad for letting you down–but I

just have to heed that intuition. I don't know what it's about–all I know is I can't go."

"I completely understand," Jeff replied (and he's the kind of spiritual guy who really does understand). "Of course you must go with your intuition."

"Can you get someone else to do the workshop with you?" I asked.

"No," he replied, "Don't worry about it. I'll just do it myself."

"Thank you so much for understanding," I said. "I feel a little embarrassed, not having any logical reason. But I've learned to heed my intuition . . . and whenever I let my head overrule my intuition, I always regret it."

"You're absolutely right," he agreed. "So don't worry about me or the workshop."

"Thanks, Jeff." And I hung up.

The next few weeks rolled by, and I just went about my normal work and forgot about the conference in Hawaii. Then one day I got an urgent call from my mother, telling me my stepfather had a heart attack and was in the hospital. I jumped in my car and drove to San Diego to be with her. I met her at the hospital, and we spent the afternoon waiting for the doctors to give us some news on his condition.

At one point, I was standing by the nurse's station talking to the nurse on duty. I glanced at the calendar on the wall behind her. Suddenly I realized this was the day I had been scheduled to conduct that workshop in Hawaii. I smiled. So this was what my intuition had been telling me; I was supposed to be here helping my family, not leading a workshop in Hawaii.

A week later when Jeff returned from the conference, I told him the story. It confirmed what we both already believed–that intuition is a unique sort of wisdom that needs to be respected and heeded.

gut truster tip

Think back to those times when you "should have trusted your intuition" and things, in fact, went awry. It's important to remember them because they can teach you just as much as the times that you trusted your intuition and things worked out well.

CHAPTER 22

Get Out of That Rut

Your time is limited; so don't waste it living someone else's life. Don't be
trapped by dogma–which is living with the results of other people's thinking.
Don't let the noise of others' opinions drown out your own inner voice. And most
important, have the courage to follow your heart and intuition.

— STEVE JOBS, CEO OF APPLE COMPUTER, INC.

It happens to all of us. That painful moment when you realize you're stuck in a rut. The job that once felt so stimulating is now boring. You've "been there, done that." It often comes on slowly. You just aren't that interested in spearheading the new company initiative. Or a new client approaches you with potential business, and you keep putting off the follow-up necessary to close the sale. You may even be out of work and unable to figure out what's next and not interested in going back to the same career you had before.

You may feel depressed, a little scared, or anxious. Those are the hallmarks of your intuition giving you a gentle nudge and saying, in effect, "Change is needed." Any time you find yourself consistently bored, drained, or depleted, look at it as a wake up-call.

Your intuition is your inner compass. It delivers the message that you need to head in a new direction and shows you the best path to get there. However, sometimes it's hard to get started. Alexander Graham Bell, the inventor of the telephone, went through many transitions in his life. He said, "When one door closes, another opens: but we often look so long and so regretfully upon the closed door that we do not see the one which has opened for us."

Time for a Change

Mark Hass was managing editor at the *Detroit News* where his staff had won a Pulitzer Prize. The world was his oyster with job offers coming from the *New York Times* and the *Wall Street Journal*. You'd think this was a high point in his life. But he said:

Instead, it was making me emotionally and physically sick.

In the 1990s, the finances of running the newspaper business began to affect the quality of the stories we were reporting. I went into journalism for all the right reasons. I wanted to afflict the comfortable and comfort the afflicted as well as make the world a better place. It was a great career . . . until it wasn't.

There was the event in the newsroom that was the last straw. It was the story about the skater Nancy Kerrigan. My paper wanted to make it into a huge tabloid feature. I wanted it to be reported more responsibly. It may seem like a small thing now, but looking back, it was an external representation of what my gut was already telling me. It was time to leave.

It's never just one thing that gets you to make a big career change. I turned 40. My father died. The career I had chosen was no longer making me happy. I was in a crisis. I knew I had to make a choice. I'm a risk taker. I think most intuitive people are.

To my friends and colleagues it may have looked like a rash decision. I wish I had let other people know what was going on. I wish I had asked for advice.

It would have made the career move a lot easier. It was a very painful time. I realize now that it didn't need to be that hard. My pride got in my way.

You just know it's time for a move. I got very focused, narrowed down the possibilities, and switched careers. I was an early believer in the Internet. I could see its potential for advertising, PR, and news. I called several colleagues in Detroit and told them my ideas about using the Web for public relations, and overnight I had two clients and began my own firm.

It wasn't a logical process. You can "overthink" some things in life. If something feels right, it probably is. Your intuition knows things. You need to be thoughtful and listen to it. It will give you good direction.

Today Mark is the CEO of Manning, Selvage and Lee (MS&L), one of the world's leading global public relations firms. He joined them in 2004 when his agency Hass Associates was acquired and merged into MS&L. "Today I trust my instincts on everything—which clients to work with, how to grow the business, and how to have as much fun as possible doing it."

The Road to Happiness

If you start work at age 20, work 40 hours a week and retire at age 65, you will have worked almost 100,000 hours. Wouldn't it be wonderful to spend those hours doing something you're passionate about, something that allows you to contribute your unique skill and interest to the world? If you don't begin now, when will you do it? John D. Rockefeller III put it this way: "The road to happiness lies in two simple principles. Find what it is that interests you and that you can do well, and when you find it, put your whole soul into it—every bit of energy and ambition and natural ability that you have."

As Mark indicated, it's not something that will likely happen overnight. All that is required of you right now is that you make a commitment to begin the process of uncovering what kind of work makes you happy. You don't have to know what it is or even how you'll make a living at it. Take it one step at a time. This is a process that will unfold in stages.

Are You Ready for a Change?

Yes No
- ❏ ❏ I want to be in a different job next year.
- ❏ ❏ I like my career but feel I'm in the wrong position.
- ❏ ❏ I long for the weekends when I can work on my hobbies or other interests.
- ❏ ❏ There are other career choices that have always fascinated me, and I'd like to check them out.
- ❏ ❏ I need to find something new that's fresh and creative.
- ❏ ❏ My work has become predictable and boring.
- ❏ ❏ I find myself daydreaming a lot about switching careers.
- ❏ ❏ I feel excited about a new career direction but can't figure out a way to earn a living at it.
- ❏ ❏ I long for a way to make a contribution to my community but don't feel I can do it in my present work.
- ❏ ❏ My life feels out of balance. (Too much work and not enough time for family, social, and personal time.)
- ❏ ❏ I'm ready to work for myself. (Or if you're already an entrepreneur . . .) I'm ready to work for someone else.

If you answered yes to most of the questions, you're definitely in a rut. Your intuition is telling you unambiguously that it's time for a career change. If you're not clear about your goals, your objective should be to *become* clear.

Rima was a client who had described herself as feeling very stuck. She had emigrated from her native Italy and spent 21 years as an Amtrak engineer in the United States. She felt justifiably proud of her ability to do well as a woman in a male-dominated industry. Several years ago we talked in my office about her confusion regarding her job. "I've always loved my work. It's given me a trade that I enjoy and I'm skilled at. But lately, I've become more and more anxious, and I'm thinking it may be time to leave."

She described waking up each morning with a feeling of dread about going to work. She was also uneasy with a new computer system her company had recently implemented. The intention of the program was to automate many of the procedures that the train drivers had previously done on their own. But to Rima it reinforced her sense of not being in control. "Every fiber in my being is telling me to get out now. But it scares me just to think about it."

She was understandably distraught over making a career change. This was something she had spent her whole life doing. She was paid well for her work, and she didn't have a clue about what else she might do to earn a living. She decided to make an appointment with a career counselor. Over the course of the next year she took several steps.

She took a TEFL (Teaching English as a Foreign Language) course with the thought that she might want to do volunteer work in Africa and India. She also found a meditation teacher who helped her find a place of calm within.

She needed that peace when days after returning to work from a vacation, the computer system failed. She described it this way: "The signal system for a train driver is supposed to work much as it does for someone driving a car at an intersection. You can proceed when there is a green light on the tracks. Yellow indicates that you prepare to slow down to stop. And a red light signifies I need to stop the train immediately.

"For whatever reason, the system went awry that day. I was barreling down the tracks at 80 miles an hour with green lights indicating it was safe sailing. All of a sudden the light turned red with no warning. This could only mean that a crash was imminent. I saw my life and those of my hundreds of passengers flash before my eyes as I slammed on the brakes.

"I successfully brought the train to a stop, adrenaline pumping through my veins. I was terrified. I was expecting an oncoming train to hit us at any moment. Inexplicably, nothing happened. The light turned green and I began moving forward again."

She later learned of the computer error and felt a small sense of relief that it hadn't been a mistake on her part. However, she was so disturbed by the incident that she took a medical leave. She reported that she kept dreaming about missing signals. The dreams (nightmares really) were so incessant and unsettling that she sought the help of a therapist. The therapist asked her a question that was to determine her next steps. "Is there a signal in your own life you're ignoring?" Her response was immediate. "Yes! Stop driving the stupid train!"

Three years later Rima is living her dream life. She owns a small studio apartment in Tuscany, travels the world doing volunteer work, and supports herself with a small stipend from the railroad. Her advice to people going through a similar life transition? "Don't be afraid. The hardest part is to make the first step. Everything else will unfold as it is supposed to. Every step happens for a reason. There are no coincidences! Listen to your intuition always. It's your guide for life."

Making the Right Turn

Many people like Rima get stuck in that limbo period between "I know it's time to leave (or change) my work" and "I don't know what I want to do next." It's an unsettling time for most people. We hate not knowing. The famous philosopher "anonymous" once said, "The bend in the road is not the end of the road unless you refuse to make the turn." Here are some steps to get you started so you can make the right turn:

- *Acknowledge it's time for a change*—You don't need to give up a job or career right now as the result of this insight. It's simply an inner step in the process of change. Consider letting friends and appropriate colleagues know what you're thinking or feeling. They may see that you possess strengths, skills, and interests that you haven't acknowledged in yourself.

- *Give yourself a period of exploration time*—Depending on your situation, this can be a few weeks to a few years. You're using this time to consult your inner compass, your intuition. Of the possibilities in front of you, what feels exciting? Be willing to explore interests that may not make immediate sense in terms of a career choice. Within your dreams, interests, and aspirations you'll find opportunity. It's as if your intuition gives you clues about the best path to follow even though your limited logical mind may not know where you're headed!

- *Commit to taking action steps*—Motivational speaker and author Tony Robbins once observed, "You see, in life, lots of people know what to do, but few people actually do what they know. Knowing is not enough! You must take action." What are three things you could do this month that would give you information about your interest? Perhaps you could take a class, read a book, make an appointment with a career coach, or talk to someone who has a similar goal. It doesn't have to be a huge risk. When you commit to action, your intuition can begin to guide you. It puts options, possibility, and hope in your path.

- *Ask your intuition open-ended questions*—These might include "What would I enjoy doing for work?" "What next steps can I take that will lead me in the right direction?" "Who can I talk with that will help me with these choices?" "What could I do that would help others and be fun for me?" As you go about your day, pay attention to any inner nudges or impulses from your intuition that points you in a new direction.

Still feeling confused? Turn the page. In the next chapter I'll give you some tools you can use to team up with your intuition and discover a new direction.

gut truster tip

Your intuition is your inner compass. It lets you know that you need to head in a new direction and shows you the best path to get there. Pay attention to the cues and clues that it may be time for a change, and then take action.

CHAPTER 23

Dealing with Setbacks

For every failure, there's an alternative course of action. You just have to find it. When you come to a roadblock, take a detour.

— MARY KAY ASH, FOUNDER OF MARY KAY COSMETICS

Gail Kauranen Jones admits she was completely burned out. She had been working in a high-pressure PR agency garnering major media exposure for her high-tech accounts. She finally left to start her own agency, hoping that the change would help her create more work-life balance.

Already successful by the time she was 26, she threw all of her energy into her new company, continuing to create a lot of new business and winning accolades from happy clients. But, after several years, she realized that the PR business wasn't for her. She was tired from the long hours, the demands of her clients, and the unending pursuit of media attention. She made the decision to sell her business.

I was so exhausted by the time I made the determination to sell that I was desperate to get out of the business. In retrospect, the fact that I had let myself

*get that burned out was a major factor in my not listening to my intuition. I
spoke to a business broker and also told my staff to be on the lookout for a
potential buyer. A week later, one of my employees, David, offered to introduce
me to an ad agency owner who was interested in talking to me about buying
my business so she could expand into PR. His words were, "She's honorable."*

*I met with her several days later. My first impression? I didn't like her. That
should have been a major sign that something was wrong, but I allowed
David's belief in her to override my own good sense. Another flag went up
when I introduced her to my anchor client. After the meeting they indicated
they didn't want the deal to go through. They were uncomfortable as well.
Because I was so desperate to get out, I ignored each cautionary message my
intuition sent forth and there were many.*

*Despite all those gut responses that told me to run in the other direction, I sold
my business to her. It was a financial and emotional disaster. I had to bring
her to court three times in five years. Each time I won. The last time, the court
again ruled in my favor. She filed for bankruptcy at the same time.*

*I'm someone who sees the positive in everything. Throughout all of this
turmoil, I was guided to a new career I'm quite passionate about–helping
people through significant life transitions. Starting a coaching practice three
years ago was an example of listening to my gut. I had an old garden shed in
my backyard, which I always dreamed of converting to a studio for writing and
working one-on-one with people.*

*One night I awoke from a dream with these words: "Build it and they will
come." Four months later, I hired a contractor who rebuilt the shed into a
sacred, nurturing space from which I launched my practice. Coaching is often
done over the phone. However, almost all my clients love to have their session
at my studio because of the tranquility–it overlooks a five-acre meadow, and
the studio itself is surrounded by gorgeous perennial gardens that I created. I
feel so grateful. Truly listening to my intuition has brought me peace.*

How Do You Know It's Intuition?

One of the questions I'm asked most frequently is "How do
you know whether it's your fear speaking or your intuition trying

to warn you away from something?" It's an excellent question and one that doesn't have a pat answer. Gail struggled with this issue when she was deciding whether to sell her business to a competitor. Here are some factors to consider:

A Small Amount of Anxiety Is Normal

If we're honest, we all experience a degree of fear when we decide to do something new. A change will likely require that you develop new skills and become more proficient with ones you already have. You're moving outside of your comfort zone into unknown territory.

Is your apprehension more pronounced than it normally would be given the change you're anticipating? You're the only one who can answer that. Think back to other times of transition in your life. How did you feel as you were going through that? Was your intuition giving you the go-ahead then? Did you trust it? How did it work out?

Just Focus on What's Next

Most decisions don't require a flying leap of faith. How could you take some small steps toward your decision? For example, you may be contemplating a career change. Do some information gathering. This might be a class you take, a colleague you speak to, or a book you read. If you're still feeling motivated and excited about the change, that's your intuition giving you a green light. Take a bigger step.

If, like Gail, you're hitting roadblocks or continuing to have uneasy feelings, pay attention! Depending on the situation, you may simply need to take a detour or just stop where you are and not move forward for the time being.

It May Not Be the Right Time

Intuition doesn't always give a clear yes or no. Sometimes it gives a qualified maybe. The implications of this message are that progress appears stalled. I have a tendency to be rather impatient. However, over the years I've learned that when I can be patient and wait, things have a way of working out. When I push the envelope and try to force things to happen, I find I've stepped out of the flow and ease that usually characterize intuitively inspired decisions and action.

Be Clear about the Outcome You Want

In Gail's story her initial goal was to sell the business to an appropriate buyer and to do it in such a way that she'd have enough money to transition easily into a new career. Admittedly, because she was fatigued and overwhelmed, she allowed the goal to become simply "sell the business."

The writer Aldous Huxley said, "When life appears to be working against you, when your luck is down, when the supposedly wrong people show up, or when you slip up and return to old, self-defeating habits, recognize the signs that you're out of harmony with intention."

If you're feeling fearful or anxious about a course of action, step back and ask yourself if you're clear about what you want. Like Gail, you may be headed in a direction you don't really want to go. If that's the case, take a break, slow down, and rethink what you truly want.

What to Do If You're Off Track

If You Get off Track, Be Willing to Change

As Yogi Berra said, "If you come to a fork in the road, take it!" What are you doing that's on the mark? If one way doesn't work for you, be ready to go another. Many times, the road to success is found by taking a detour. Sometimes we get overly focused on getting to our goals through a well-trodden or familiar path.

It's worth noting that many of the people I interviewed for this book mentioned failures, detours, and other crises that ultimately served to get them on track. With enough distance, almost all of them were grateful for the setbacks because it allowed a whole new and more interesting life to emerge. They invariably mentioned that following their intuition was the guide that led them back to success.

Look Ahead Rather Than Back

Sometimes a shift in perspective is all it takes to get you out of a state of anxiety. I was speaking recently with a client who was contemplating going back to school for a master's degree at 53 years old. She was the director of a high-profile nonprofit organization and had been in this position for 15 years. She knew it was time to leave and yet was consumed with anxiety about whether the program she'd been accepted into was the right choice. Was her intuition telling her not to go? I suggested she think of her life a year from now and asked, "How will you feel if you're still in your current job and you didn't go back to school." Her instant reply? "Disappointed." Her response served to soften her anxiety. It made her realize that she was, in fact, heading in the right direction.

Give Yourself a Performance Review

When you've put a lot of hard work into an endeavor and it's not going as you planned, it's not easy to step back and assess the situation. Is there something that you feel you're failing at in your life? The following questions will help you put some perspective on your experience.

- What can you learn from this?
- What are you doing right?
- What outcome will make you feel you're successful?
- Where did this begin to go wrong?
- What do you wish you had done differently?
- What is your intuition telling you to do about this situation?
- What are you not listening to?
- Are there warning signs you're ignoring?
- What do you know you should do?

After answering the above questions, do you feel there's a different way to approach your project or endeavor? Depending on the issue, you have several options. You could

- quit
- persevere
- alter your course
- put the project on hold for a period of time
- try something new
- ask for advice from someone who has been successful in a similar endeavor
- work on your project part-time
- discuss the situation with others who may be involved

Which of these options feels best to you? You can choose more than one, and your intuition may present you with even more choices than those listed.

A Formula for Success

Thomas J. Watson was the founder of IBM. He was one of the richest men of his time and considered one of the world's greatest salesmen when he died in 1956. I thought his words might provide some comfort for those experiencing a setback:

Would you like me to give you a formula for success? It's quite simple, really. Double your rate of failure. You are thinking of failure as the enemy of success. But it isn't at all. You can be discouraged by failure or you can learn from it. So go ahead and make mistakes. Make all you can. Because, remember, that's where you will find success.

gut truster tip

Intuition doesn't always give a clear yes or no. Sometimes it gives a qualified maybe. When you try to force things to happen, you may find that you step out of the flow and the ease that usually characterize intuitively inspired decisions and action.

CHAPTER 24

Success Is an Inside Job

If you can dream it you can do it.

— WALT DISNEY, MOVIE PRODUCER AND FOUNDER OF DISNEYLAND AND DISNEY WORLD

Many of us take the path of least resistance in life. We're out of work, a job is offered, and we might as well take it. Or an opportunity has opened up in another department. It offers a change of pace, more money, and it's clearly a promotion. You decide you'll take it. Why not? The cliché that "if you don't know where you're going, you'll probably end up there" holds true in so many situations. We fail to check in with our intuition and ask, "Is this a good decision?" How will you know if you don't ask and if you do ask, how will you know the answer? (Aren't you glad you asked?!)

Asking What's Next

Marilyn is one of my clients. At our first meeting she explained, "I took the first job offer I received after graduating from college. Since then, I've been promoted many times, changed jobs twice, and continue to make more money and achieve significant career advancement. Everyone who knows me would say I'm successful. I'm 38 years old, married, have a mortgage and two kids to support, and it finally occurred to me that I've really never asked myself what makes my heart sing. I've just grabbed the next obvious opportunity as it came my way. No wonder I'm unhappy!"

You can sit in on our initial meeting where we discussed many of the themes in this chapter.

What's Wrong with Your Current Situation?

Often the answer to the question "what's next?" is a little too overwhelming and not easily answered. Sometimes it helps to understand what you don't want before figuring out what you do want.

Marilyn had a ready list of items that weren't working for her in her present occupation.

I don't like being in a huge corporation. I feel like a cog in a wheel. The long hours are really tough on me because I'm not spending enough time with family, friends, or even myself. I have a new boss who is a micromanager, and I'm someone who really thrives on autonomy. Also, I'm an extrovert and my current job requires spending hours at my desk doing detailed analysis.

Marilyn's comments may sound like one long whine, but asking yourself what you don't want or don't like about your current situation will provide valuable information about what you *do* want. Here are some ideas I shared with Marilyn:

Get Clear about What You Want

Look at the list of statements about what's not working in your current job. Try turning them around. Following are a few examples based on the conversation with Marilyn:

- "I no longer want to work long hours." Becomes . . .
  "I want a job where I can be home in time to see my son's afternoon baseball games." Or "I'd love to be at a company that allows me to telecommute several days a week."

- "I'm an extrovert who dislikes doing detailed analysis." Becomes . . .
  "I'd love to do work where I'm out meeting customers at least part of the week. I could also imagine coaching, speaking, or training as part of my job. Anything that gets me out with people."

Being clear about *what* you want is often the first step in being able to create it. Set aside for now the question of *how* you will get this work or job. That will come later. Don't put the cart before the horse. It's difficult to focus on *how* you're going to get someplace before figuring out *where* it is you're heading!

Begin to play around with the idea of creating something new. I jokingly tell people that if I can make a living at what *I* do, it's possible to make a living doing anything! When you discover the answer to "what" (you love to do), your intuition will provide the insight that will give you the clues to discover the "how" (to make a living at it).

Gerry Harrington, president of New Spirituality Communications, adds these words of wisdom: "Go for things that are aligned with your values, even if there's nothing like it anywhere in the world. Your heart doesn't invest in a compromise."

Say No to "Buts"

You've probably had many creative and inspirational ideas about things that you'd like to do, achieve, or accomplish. Perhaps you, like Marilyn, have had a fantasy of trying some entirely new type of work. Maybe you've daydreamed about a trip you wanted to take. Or you may have relegated a passion for something into "just a hobby" instead of allowing for the possibility you could make a living at it.

If you haven't taken action on those ideas, I'd be willing to bet you've fallen under the tyranny of a powerful word—"But." That word puts the kibosh on anything that preceded it. "I could do this, this, and this!" you think excitedly. That's your intuition serving up some creative and innovative ideas that will point you in a new and successful direction.

Unfortunately, your logical mind joins in at just that moment with "But how can you do that? You can't! Your idea is nonsense. It's too hard (expensive, requires more education or training, blah, blah, blah). Here's an example of a "yes-but" that Marilyn came up with: "I'd love to be more involved with customer service training. The idea of making us more customer friendly really appeals to me. But . . . I'd have to go back to school to get a degree."

Shift Your Thinking

There's nothing wrong with the fact that your logical mind jumps in and wants to have some input into how you'll achieve these random hopes and dreams. After all, it has a role to play in helping you succeed! However, you don't want it to dampen your enthusiasm and inspirational sparks by leaping in too soon. Try saying such things as "Let me be open to possibilities." "What steps could I take to make this happen?" "Where can I begin?" "If this idea were possible, what would I do next?"

Make the First Step a Small Step

The trick to breaking the habit of defeatist thinking is two-fold: (1) just begin and (2) start small. Take a first step toward what you feel excited about and then take another one and another one. Remain centered in the present. You don't have to know exactly *how* your dreams will manifest themselves. Trust your inner direction from your intuition. When you follow your passion, excitement, and inner knowing, you'll discover what makes you happy and fulfilled. When you know what you want, there's a clear path to achieve it. Your guidance will show you the way.

Keep an Intuitive Career Ideas Journal

Jotting down ideas as they come to you is one of the most helpful ways to open our mind to allow intuitive idea generation. Below are some questions to get you started. Clients have approached this list in varied ways. Marilyn bought a purse-size notebook, and every day she focused on answering just one question, writing down the ideas as they came to her. Others have taken a several-day retreat where they could take time with their answers. Whatever works for you is fine.

What are your gifts?

- What life achievements or accomplishments have made you feel proud?
- What abilities do you have that people praise?
- What tasks or skills come easily to you? Make a list of things you do well.
- What were you good at as a child?
- If someone were to give your eulogy, what contributions would they say you have made to the world?

What are you passionate about?

- What are you doing when you lose track of time?
- If you had enough money to take a year off, what would you do with your free time?
- Is there something you want to devote your life to?
- How can you help others by doing what you enjoy?
- If you could make one contribution to the world before you die, what would it be?
- What do you want to teach others?
- What excites or angers you most about our world?

What are your values?

- What matters most to you? Consider things like autonomy, humanity, creativity, kindness, power, wealth, spirituality, knowledge, leadership, community, beauty, and intellectual pursuits.
- Think of someone you admire. What is it about his life that you appreciate? What values do you think he holds?

What's fun for you?

- Make a list of 20, 50, or 100 things you love to do.
- How would you spend your ideal day/week/month/year?
- If you were to win the lottery and money were no longer an object, what would you do?
- Do you enjoy doing things by yourself? With a partner? A team?
- What kind of setting do you like to be in? Are you an outdoor person or more comfortable behind a desk? Consider your surroundings when imagining your fun, ideal life.

As you look at your answers, are there any themes that emerged? Were there any "aha" moments that caught you by surprise? Once you have your list of accomplishments, competencies, values, and passions, there are a few more steps. The answer to the question, How can I do something I enjoy and make a living at it? may not come overnight.

What happened to Marilyn? She stayed with her current company and pitched them on a new position. She's now a customer service liaison. She follows up with current customers to make sure they've had a successful experience with her company. She communicates suggestions for improvements as well as praises back to headquarters. She reports she couldn't be happier!

Patience

One of the qualities I believe we must develop in order to use our intuition wisely is patience. The changes that Marilyn ultimately made didn't happen overnight. She quotes Napoleon Hill, author of the classic book *Think and Grow Rich:* "Patience, persistence and perspiration make an unbeatable combination for success."

gut truster tip

Try saying things like the following:

"Let me be open to possibilities."

"What steps could I take to make this happen?"

"Where can I begin?"

"If this idea were possible, what would I do next?"

Your intuition will begin to supply the answers.

Appendix:
Gut Truster Techniques

*The important thing is not to stop questioning. Curiosity has its own
reason for existing. One cannot help but be in awe when one
contemplates the mysteries of eternity, of life, of the
marvelous structure of reality. It is enough if one tries merely to
comprehend a little of this mystery every day. Never lose a holy curiosity.*

— ALBERT EINSTEIN, PHYSICIST

There are an infinite number of techniques you can use to tap
into the wisdom of your intuition. I've described many thus far.
Following is a collection of some of my other favorites:

1. The Intuitive Ideas Log
2. Not Your Typical Coin Toss
3. When Is It Time for Something New?
4. Small Steps Lead to Big Strides
5. How Do You Know You're on the Right Track?
6. You've Got "I-Mail"
7. The Magic of Metaphor
8. Tapping into Your Inner Genius
9. Thirteen Ways to Inspire Creativity and Intuition in Your Team
10. Double-check Your Gut Check
11. Seven Ways to Jump-start Your Intuition When You Have Five Minutes or Less
12. Intuitive Hiring
13. What Are You Ready to Act On?
14. The Gut Trusters Checklist

We're all different and have diverse ways of experiencing the gentle prompting of our inner guidance. My hope is that you'll find several that will become tried and true for you.

I also hope you'll befriend and nurture your intuition. Treat those random thoughts, gut feelings, instincts, dreams, images, and nudges as if they were gifts from a wise friend. Your intuition always has your best interests at heart and will continually point you in the direction of success and happiness.

1. The Intuitive Ideas Log

*Intuition is so powerful that it has been studied and written about
for thousands of years by some of the greatest men and women in history.
When you begin to use it regularly and systematically,
there is virtually nothing that you cannot accomplish.*
— **BRIAN TRACY, BEST-SELLING AUTHOR, CONSULTANT, AND SPEAKER**

Keeping an intuition journal is a terrific way to expand your proficiency. Keep your ideas written in one place, whether it's on your PDA, a Word document, or a spiral-bound notebook.

Many people have found it helpful to create "intuition check-in" points during the day. This is a time set aside, often at the beginning of the workday, to check in with their intuition.

- Sit in a quiet place or simply close the door to your office and hold your calls.
- Consider your concerns, issues, decisions, and challenges for the day. Write them out in your journal. Give each one a separate page.
- Close your eyes and take several slow, deep breaths and center yourself.
- Bring each of your concerns to mind one-by-one. Ask questions such as, "what should I know about . . . ?" Or make a statement, "I need information about . . ."
- Pay attention to intuitive response(s). Remember, intuition doesn't usually come in fully formed sentences. A picture, phrase, feeling, or a symbolic image can all be equally valuable.
- Write all responses—even brief fragments—into your journal. Try not to edit or analyze your answers during this exercise. That can come later.

Don't be discouraged if you're not immediately flooded with insightful wisdom. Intuitive insights have a way of arriving when you least expect them, often coming to mind later in the day. When a great idea comes, make a note of it! An intuition journal is a way to invite even more valuable hunches and instincts.

Check back with it frequently. You may find that an answer that didn't make sense earlier in the month provides exactly the information you need now.

2. Not Your Typical Coin Toss

No great discovery was ever made without a bold guess.

— SIR ISAAC NEWTON, MATHEMATICIAN AND PHYSICIST

This is a great technique to use when the stakes aren't too high. I wouldn't necessarily use this method for major decisions such as whether to sell the company, quit your job, or move across the continent. But then, that's just me!

1. Think about a decision you're trying to make. Form it in your mind as a yes or no question. Examples are: "Should I take the position with XYZ Corporation?" "Is this the right time to ask for a raise?" "Is it important that I attend the annual association meeting next month?"
2. Take a coin and flip it. Heads indicates yes. Tails indicates no. Okay, what was the answer?
3. Think about how you felt about the answer. Were you disappointed? Relieved? Did you get a thrill of excitement through your body or a knot of fear in your stomach? Admit it, did you immediately want to flip the coin two more times and try for best two out of three? (Or have you actually done that already?)

Any of these responses is an example of your intuition speaking to you. You know the answer. It's the one you wanted in the first place. Your response after you tossed the coin gave you more information about the answer to your question.

So often we expect our intuition to speak like Darth Vader in *Star Wars* booming out, "Yes! Take that job!" It's more likely that the message will come through subtle feelings, an inner nudge, a physical sensation. When you learn to pay attention to these inner clues and act on them, they can be as loud and clear as any booming voice.

3. When Is It Time for Something New?

A definition of insanity: doing the same thing over and over again and expecting different results.

— RITA MAE BROWN, AUTHOR

Life is full of transitions. The job that was once so compelling now feels draining. The new initiative you were thrilled to champion has become old school. Doors of opportunity used to fly open and now you can't seem to find the key. These are all important messages from your inner guidance that change is needed.

It can be a scary time because often we have to let go of what's not working before making room for anything new. Most of us are more comfortable when we have clear goals and an action plan for success. If you're finding that creative, innovative ideas and new direction are not coming to mind, you may have to clear out some space to allow room for a fresh approach.

If you've read this far in the book, you know that intuition is a clear guide to show you the most direct path to success. It can also tell you when it's time to change direction. When you're feeling positive and excited, that's your intuition giving you a thumbs-up. Following is a list of intuitive indicators that tell you you're headed in the wrong direction or that a change is needed.

Yes No
- ❑ ❑ I'm overwhelmed.
- ❑ ❑ I feel depressed.
- ❑ ❑ I've worked at something for a long time, and nothing seems to go right.
- ❑ ❑ People are not responding positively to my efforts.
- ❑ ❑ I'm having trouble sleeping.
- ❑ ❑ I'm constantly worried.
- ❑ ❑ I'm trying too hard.
- ❑ ❑ I frequently procrastinate.

Yes No

❑ ❑ I don't have a clear sense of direction.

❑ ❑ I've lost confidence in myself and my abilities.

❑ ❑ I feel as if I constantly have to push to make things happen.

❑ ❑ I've lost my motivation.

❑ ❑ This endeavor is no longer fun and stimulating.

❑ ❑ I'm frequently anxious.

❑ ❑ I'm taking a lot of action steps to no avail.

❑ ❑ I have recurrent accidents or illnesses.

❑ ❑ Nothing I try seems to work.

❑ ❑ I feel as though I have to do it all myself.

❑ ❑ I'm frequently tired.

❑ ❑ Nothing seems interesting.

Clearly some of the above may indicate depression or some other illness. If you're experiencing many of these feelings and thoughts, you may want to make sure you don't have a medical condition. For the rest of you, if you checked off five or more boxes, your intuition is trying to point you in a new direction. Not sure what to do next? Read on!

4. Small Steps Lead to Big Strides

We go in the direction we face, and we face the direction we think.

— JIM ROHN, BUSINESS PHILOSOPHER, SPEAKER, AND AUTHOR

When you're clear you're headed in the wrong direction, the obvious question is, "What's next?" If you're like most people, you don't want to take any action until you have a crystal clear goal. Many of my clients call me when they're in that particular limbo state. It's uncomfortable to feel stuck.

I believe that intuition not only tells you when you're on the wrong path but it also provides the clues to get you back on track.

What are some things you enjoy? Make a plan to do at least one of those things every day. Think of those small pleasures as part of the direction your intuition is providing to get you back on the right track. This may not make logical sense to you, but do it anyway. What have you got to lose besides a few moments away from feeling bad? Begin to notice what you feel excited about. That's a clue about what to pursue.

Focus on where you want to go. If a project has failed, you're out of work, or experiencing some other form of setback, it's all too easy to rehash the past. Most of the time that's wasted energy and will only serve to keep you feeling down. If you don't have a clear goal, focus on what you do know. These might be such objectives as, "I want a position where I'll have autonomy." "I want to feel excited about my work again." Or "I want some clear direction." When you can state what you want, your intuition will begin to provide guidance to get you there.

Take small steps every day. If you're in a major life transition, you may be feeling overwhelmed and lacking direction. Instead of trying to figure out the next big goal or plan, take smaller steps. Make your first goal figuring out what you want to do. What might that look like on a day-to-day basis?

- Take a class in a subject that interests you.
- Read a book on the subject.
- Talk to someone who has the type of job you're curious about.
- Speak with someone who has had a problem similar to the one you're facing.
- Hang out with people who are encouraging and upbeat.
- Go on a retreat (and take your intuition journal!).
- Have lunch with someone whose advice you value.
- Volunteer doing something you enjoy.
- Join a group or association that relates to your area of interest.

What are you doing that's on the mark? What are you doing that feels off the mark? If one way doesn't work for you, be ready to go to another. Many times the road to success is found by taking a detour.

Cultivate the attitude of a wish fulfilled. Success is waiting for you. Use the power of visualization and affirmation to vividly imagine, sense, and feel the life you want to live.

I love this quote by Michael Angier: "A successful day: to learn something new; to laugh at least 10 times; to lift someone up; to make progress on a worthy goal; to practice peace and patience; to do something nice for yourself and another; to appreciate and be grateful for all your blessings."

5. How Do You Know You're on the Right Track?

The main reason intuition is so important is this: It is a clear sign that you are connecting with your inner spiritual guidance system. Intuition is a direct signal from your deepest self that you are navigating from your true center."

— DRS. GAY HENDRICKS AND KATE LUDEMAN, AUTHORS OF *THE CORPORATE MYSTIC*

People often tell me they're "not intuitive." Our inner guidance system is really not all that complicated. Simply put, if you're feeling good and things are working out and you're in the flow of life, that's your intuition telling you to continue with whatever you're doing. Conversely, if things are stuck, difficult, and you feel bad, your intuition is indicating a change of course is needed.

Need a checklist to know whether you're on the right track? Here it is:

Yes No

❑ ❑ I enjoy my work and life.

❑ ❑ My connections with friends, colleagues, and family are strong.

❑ ❑ I'm proud of my accomplishments.

❑ ❑ I'm in the flow. Things happen fairly easily in my life without a lot of pushing and effort.

❑ ❑ I help others through my product, service, or simply by my example.

❑ ❑ I feel confident.

❑ ❑ I feel creative and challenged by my work.

❑ ❑ I'm easily able to shift direction if something isn't working.

❑ ❑ I listen to my intuition and follow its wisdom.

❑ ❑ Doors of opportunity seem to open effortlessly.

❑ ❑ People respond positively to me and my work.

❑ ❑ I like what I do.

❑ ❑ I wake up each day and look forward to it.

❑ ❑ I feel motivated to do my best work.

❑ ❑ I have a good work-life balance.

Yes No

❏   ❏   I feel positive about the future.

❏   ❏   I sleep well at night.

❏   ❏   I allow time for creative, personal, and/or spiritual interests.

If you checked five or more you're on the right path. You may
not experience all of the above all of the time! If you do, your intuition is giving you a pat on the back and encouragement to keep
going!

If you're faced with a choice about a new project, job, assignment, or direction, put it to the intuition test. Here are two
questions:

1. Is this something I want to do now?
2. Am I excited or energized by the thought of taking it on?

You'll know in your gut the right answer. It usually comes instantly without a lot of thought. If you feel you should do it or feel
duty-bound to say yes, wait. Try the answer, "Let me think about
this and get back to you." Then spend some time with any of the
exercises you've learned in this book to determine what your intuition is telling you about this decision.

Remember, when you say no to what you don't want, you're
allowing space in your life for something better.

6. You've Got I-Mail!

If you feel the desire that there is something that you
want to do and it keeps presenting itself over and over,
listen to your inner voice–test the concept, do the pros
and cons, and then damn the torpedoes, full speed ahead.

— VAL JORDAN, FOUNDER OF JORDAN AND JORDAN FINANCIAL SERVICES FIRM

Betsy Wiersma remembers the day an intuitive message just popped into her mind.

I love glass beads and silver and making jewelry. I also love big ideas and saving little pieces of the world whenever possible. One day I simply heard the words, "Make HOPE Bracelets (Helping Organizations Promote Education) and they will help people around the world."

This voice was more a command than a request! It was like when you hear "You've got mail!" on your computer. This time it was "I-Mail." My intuition was talking to me. From the power of that information came the plan and the connections to raise $250,000 for a school in Ethiopia selling glass bead bracelets. I guess I was open to direction and listening for that intuitive voice.

We've all had those times when we've thought and thought about a decision and just can't seem to land on the right answer. It's as if we're so caught up in logic, facts, and data that we can't see the proverbial trees for the forest. During those periods when you feel stuck, listen for I-Mail. It often comes, as it did for Betsy, in a word, a phrase, or a sudden insight.

You know you've received I-Mail when you have an "aha" moment. An idea or concept that wasn't in your mind a split second before is now there. These seem to come when you least expect them and usually not when you're engaged in serious and solemn thought.

What can you do to invite this kind of intuitive message? Get clear about what you want and be open to the guidance. Betsy told me she was looking for something fun and creative that would allow her to give back to the world.

Step 1: What Do You Want?

Here's a list of examples. I want a winning idea for:

- The theme for our annual meeting
- My next direct mail piece
- Our new ad campaign
- Approaching the acquisition committee
- Boosting sales at our winter conference

Step 2: Chill Out!

What do you enjoy that's creative and relatively mindless? Do it. For some it's knitting, for others it might be completing a crossword puzzle, cooking, or playing a musical instrument. You want to create a period of downtime when you're simply enjoying yourself and not thinking about your problem or concern. Be advised that the I-Mail message may not pop into your mind during this creative interval but may happen when you least expect it at some point during the day.

Step 3: Listen

Intuitive insights have a distinct feel. Remember the ad campaign for V-8 Juice? The actors had little thought balloons that said, "I could have had a V-8!" I-Mail is like that. People often describe them as a "pop" of inspiration or ideas. You can't force them to happen. You create an environment that allows them to occur. Just like that a wonderful idea will come to you and then you, too, can say, "I've got I-Mail!"

7. The Magic of Metaphor

The greatest thing by far is to be a master of metaphor. It is the one thing that cannot be learned from others; and it is also a sign of genius, since a good metaphor implies intuitive perception of the similarity in dissimilars.

— ARISTOTLE

The use of metaphors is a wonderful way to unleash your creative muse. A metaphor is simply a different way of thinking about something. Using metaphors to compare your situation to something else is one of the easiest techniques to get ideas flowing.

Roger Von Oech wrote one of the classic books on creativity: *A Whack on the Side of the Head.* He states, "There is always a connection between the random thing you select and your problem—and your job is to find it. We humans are quite good at finding patterns and meaning in the world around us—even if none were intended. Whatever you find will add insight into your problem."

Step 1: Define the Problem

Frame the problem as a question. For example, consumer focus groups have revealed that your product doesn't have sufficient brand recognition. Your question becomes, "How can we increase brand recognition?"

Step 2: Define Your Key Concept

Start with the most basic idea for your product. What is it that you most want your customer or buyer to know? This might be "healthy" or "cost effective" or "innovative" or "low carb."

Step 3: Create a Symbolic Representation of Your Key Concept

You can use words or visuals. Try crayons, paint, or colored pens. Rip pictures out of magazines if that helps get your creative juices flowing! Draw, write, or paste images that reflect the best metaphor of the benefit you want to communicate.

Step 4: Use Sentence Completion

Remember Tom Hanks's famous line in the movie *Forrest Gump?* "Life is like a box of chocolates." Similes are comparisons between two objects using the words "like" or "as." A simile can help you find a metaphor.

- "This brand, service, or product is like_____"
- "The benefit to the consumer of this brand, product, or service is like _____"

A metaphor can be used to characterize the brand's personality. A branding campaign for a healthy fast-food company uses the visual metaphor of a runner, for example, to characterize the company's product as quick and healthy.

Step 5: Choose a Random Object or Action

To generate some creative ideas, compare your product or service to an arbitrary object or a situation. For example: How is your brand similar to

- running a race?
- doing stand-up comedy?
- being a politician?
- political office?
- downhill skiing?
- being a new parent of twins?

- an Internet dating service?
- being a motivational speaker?

Step 6: Reflect and Choose

What have you come up with so far? Are there images, feelings, concepts that have grabbed you? That's your intuition speaking. It informs you of the best ideas based on all your creative input. Now do what Nike suggests in its ad campaigns and "Just do it!"

8. Tapping into Your Inner Genius

When you close your doors, and make darkness within, remember never to say that you are alone, for you are not alone; nay, God is within, and your genius is within. And what need have they of light to see what you are doing?

— EPICTETUS, ROMAN PHILOSOPHER

Masaru Ibuka, founder and chairman of Japan's Sony Corporation, was asked in an interview, "What is the secret of your success?" He said he had a ritual. Preceding a business decision, he would drink herbal tea. Before he drank, he asked himself, "Should I make this deal or not?" If the tea gave him indigestion, he wouldn't make the deal. "I trust my gut, and I know how it works," he said. "My mind is not that smart, but my body is."

Ibuka discovered a way to tap into *his* inner genius. How can you discover *yours*? Think of a decision you made recently that you're unequivocally sure was a great choice. Perhaps it resulted in a big sale or customer accolades or simply gave you great personal satisfaction. Whatever the situation, bring it to mind.

Most likely there were strong logical reasons for making this decision. However, there was probably a strong intuitive reason as well. You want to become familiar with how your intuition conveys a "yes" response. Spend a few moments checking in with yourself. Here are some questions to ask:

- How did you know it was right?
- Where did you geel it in your body?
- If you close your eyes, what image or images come to mind when you think of this choice?
- Was there a word or words you heard in your mind when you were contemplating it?

- What made this decision stand out over other options you could have chosen?
- How would you know if you were to get this similar "go ahead" message from your intuition in the future?

You may want to repeat this exercise with a bad choice you made. While possibly more painful to examine, it will nonetheless provide helpful clues about how your intuition communicates to you that you're heading in the wrong direction.

You're the expert on yourself and your intuitive responses. It's as if your inner genius has its own unique language with which it conveys its wisdom. Your job is to be a skilled translator.

9. Thirteen Ways to Inspire Creativity and Intuition in Your Team

Everyone who has ever taken a shower has had an idea. It's the person who gets out of the shower, dries off, and does something about it that makes a difference.

— **NOLAN BUSHNELL, FOUNDER OF ATARI**

1. Post creative thinking articles on your company intranet, on bulletin boards, employee newsletters, and in e-mails.
2. Hire people with a broad range of interests and aptitudes. Look for individuals whose hobbies include music, art, or other creative pursuits.
3. Encourage interdepartment conversation and meetings. Foster conversation between the creative types and the analytic types. Understand that it takes all kinds to make your company strong.
4. Acknowledge great ideas and innovations on a regular basis through awards, gift certificates, or other form of appreciation.
5. Establish a CCO (chief creative officer) position. One of the CCO's duties would be to hold informal lunchtime discussion groups on the topic of creativity and innovation.
6. Establish a quiet room in your company. Encourage employees to use it for individual brainstorming, meditation, or writing.
7. Actively promote the use of intuition by encouraging people to take risks and try new ideas.
8. Make sure at least some of your meetings are nonstructured. Foster brainstorming, a playful approach, and outside-of-box thinking.
9. Encourage initiative through suggestion boxes, an open door policy, and receptiveness to new ideas.
10. Promote the use of creativity, meditation, and intuition seminars either by paying for employees to go to programs

outside the company or by bringing in trainers and consultants on the topic.

11. Buy books on creativity, innovation, and intuition for your senior managers or make them available in a company library.

12. Encourage the development of blogs or online discussion on the topic of creative ideas for your company's services or products.

13. Before your next meeting ask everyone to contribute a written solution to the problem or challenge you're facing. Begin the meeting by reading the responses aloud. Keep the focus on the solutions, and you'll generate more intuitive responses (and have a constructive and positive meeting!).

10. Double-check Your Gut Check

Believe it is possible to solve your problem. Tremendous things happen to the believer. So believe the answer will come. It will.

— NORMAN VINCENT PEALE, AUTHOR OF *THE POWER OF POSITIVE THINKING*

"Is intuition always accurate?" It's a question I'm often asked and my answer is always the same: Intuition is 100 percent accurate but your interpretation might be wrong. That may sound like a cop-out answer, but we're human and so we translate the intuitive information we receive through fallible human filters. These might include wishful thinking, fear, preconceived ideas and beliefs, concern about what others may think, or how our ideas might be judged.

As noted previously in the book, intuition is a gift, but it's also a skill. To become proficient at it you have to practice. If you were training to be a concert pianist or an Olympic athlete, you wouldn't expect to be perfect the first time you practiced. Intuition is no different. But how do you practice such a subtle skill?

- *Recognize your decision-making style.* If using intuition is new to you, begin at the beginning. Think about how you've made decisions in the past. Do you recognize some of the ways your intuition may have communicated with you? What decisions have worked out well and which ones haven't? What role did intuition play (or not play?)
- *Pay attention to the first option that comes to mind.* Research shows that our first impressions are often the best. They are usually the ones uncontaminated by fear, anxiety, wishful thinking, or a need to impress others. You can overrule this choice. However, if you need to use your intuition to make a quick decision, it's often best to go with that first impulse.
- *Keep in touch with your intuition as you move ahead.* Many decisions involve a number of small choices followed by an action step. For example, after doing some research, you've

decided it's time to add a new product line to your company. Your gut feeling gives you the "go ahead," but be sure to periodically check in with your intuition as you talk to vendors, salespeople, customer service, and so on. Is there any place along the way where you get a warning sign or are you still getting a green light?

- *Filter out strong emotions.* Whenever you're making a decision it helps to make a choice from a neutral, clear place. As noted previously, meditation, or simply focusing within, is conducive to tapping that well of inner wisdom. It's also helpful to be aware of any intense feelings that you have. Meditation teachers suggest you focus on your breathing and simply notice thoughts and emotions and let them go as best you can. Asking for intuitive impressions from this impartial place in your psyche will yield the best results.

11. Seven Ways to Jump-start Your Intuition When You Have Five Minutes or Less

What is truth? A difficult question; but I have solved it for myself by saying that it is what what the voice within tells you.

— MAHATMA GANDHI, INDIAN SPIRITUAL AND POLITICAL LEADER

1. *Meditate.* Simply calm your mind by focusing on your breathing. Repeat a word or phrase that makes you feel relaxed such as "peace," "It's all good," or "calm." Buddhists call this mindfulness. When we slow down for even a few moments, we cultivate our creativity, intuition, and inner peace.

2. *Choose the right questions.* Framing the questions to evoke more than a yes or no answer will elicit a more informative response. For example, "How can we get more people to sign up for our seminar next month?" Or "What could we do to create more brand recognition of product X?" Spend your remaining time writing any and all answers that pop into your mind. Don't censor or judge the responses until you've completed the exercise.

3. *Ask for an image.* If you're trying to make a decision about something and your logical, rational mind is running amok, close your eyes and ask for a symbolic picture of the solution. Intuitive answers often come through a visual representation.

4. *Get moving.* Simply standing up and moving will bring more oxygen to your brain and help you think more clearly. Put your work on hold and go for a brisk walk. Chances are good that simply getting away from your desk and taking your focus off your problem will generate a creative idea or two.

5. *Daydream.* Think about the challenge, decision, or problem you're facing. In your mind's eye visualize yourself in a situation where you're dealing with this issue and expect an

answer. Perhaps someone comes up to you and provides the solution in a conversation. Or you might see a book, banner, note, or some other communication that gives you a clue to the response you're seeking. While it may seem odd or silly, you'd be surprised how many wonderful solutions come forth this way.

6. *Notice how it feels.* You're trying to make a decision about whether to invest in an expensive new piece of equipment your factory manager is asking for. He's presented a good case with all the facts and figures. You're still not sure. Close your eyes and imagine saying "yes." How does that decision feel? How do you feel emotionally? Heavy, weighty, depressing feelings generally indicate "Don't go with this." Up, energizing, enthusiastic, positive emotions point to an affirmative response.

7. *What does your body say?* The ancient Chinese believed that wisdom resides in the stomach. An early example of "trust your gut" perhaps? If your stomach becomes nervous at the thought of a particular direction, pay attention. Other physical sensations may provide clues as well. Perhaps you break into a sweat when faced with a choice you know isn't right. Others might feel a tingly zing up their spine. On the other hand, a warm, cozy feeling might indicate you're heading in the right direction. Only you know your body and can read its signs. When you're comfortable translating its messages you'll have tapped into your inner genius.

12. Intuitive Hiring

Intuition is the supralogic that cuts out all the routine processes of thought and leaps straight from the problem to the answer.

— ROBERT GRAVES, IRISH NOVELIST

Whether you're trying to decide on a new hire or a promotion of an internal candidate, your intuition can guide you.

What's Your Ideal Outcome?

Example: My perfect candidate for the floor manager position would be

- a great team leader.
- an exemplary communicator.
- detail oriented.
- comfortable with diversity.

Focus Within

Gather the list of résumés or candidate names you're considering for this position. Shut the door to your office and hold your calls. Close your eyes, take a deep breath, and center yourself. "Who is the right person to hire?"

Intuition answers by one or all of the following:

- The name of the ideal hire leaps to mind.
- You have a strong positive feeling about one of the applicants.
- You have a physical sensation such as a rush of energy that indicates a positive response.
- You simply *know* the answer.

13. What Are You Ready to Act On?

I believe that every minute we're awake our life is sending us messages about what we should be doing, where we should be headed.

— EILEEN FISHER, WOMEN'S CLOTHING DESIGNER

Sometimes you become confused because you can't figure out how to get from where you are to where you want to go. You may also feel stuck because something doesn't feel right. This is when your intuition can help. Maybe all that's required is a small step, not a huge leap. Quite often when you take a step forward, more information becomes available to you.

Many people report that as they make an intuitive choice toward what proves to be a correct decision, events begin flowing easily, doors to opportunity open, and coincidences begin to occur.

Which of the following feels like the next best step?

- I need to gather more information.
- I'd like to call _____ and ask for her input.
- This decision should be delayed.
- I'm ready to act on ____ but not ____.
- I'd like to make a list of pros and cons.
- I'd like to ask __ and ___ to brainstorm with me.
- I'm not comfortable with the direction we're headed and need to slow this down.

What small step(s) can I take today?

14. The Gut Trusters Checklist

Intuition is one of the most important abilities we can cultivate . . . It is becoming
necessary for a comprehensive personal and global perspective.
— JAGDISH PARIKH, COFOUNDER OF THE WORLD BUSINESS ACADEMY

You've got a big decision to make. Here's a checklist of the top 12 ideas to use that will allow you to quickly access your intuitive insights.

1. State your desired outcome. It can be as general as "motivate my sales team" or as specific as "I want to partner with the Smith Company."
2. If you have time, immerse yourself in information about your subject.
3. Use your logical mind to analyze the options available to you and then give it over to your intuition to make the best choice.
4. Ask your intuition a question: "What should I do about . . . ?" "How can I . . . ?" "What do I need to know about . . . ?" These are all good examples of ways to phrase a question to evoke intuitive information.
5. Take a break. Get away from your desk and preferably out of the office for at least five minutes.
6. Quiet your mind with a breathing exercise or a simple meditation. Clear your mind of distractions. Listen for the answers.
7. Make a hypothetical choice. Does it feel right in your gut? Do you feel energized by the decision? Can you see the successful completion of this plan of action? If the answer is yes to all, you're on the right track. If not, choose again.
8. Close your eyes and ask for an image or symbolic picture that represents the answer.

9. Take out your notebook or laptop and brainstorm a number of possible options. At the end of ten minutes, go through your list. Which of the choices feel best to you?

10. Let go of the "what ifs." It's possible to endlessly obsess over possible consequences of your decisions until it clouds intuitive vision.

11. What do you know for sure? What pops into your mind when you ask that question?

12. Go with what you know. Take a bold step and then another! Keep tuning into your intuition and asking questions each step along the way.

My prediction? You're going to continue on the path to success by trusting your gut and growing your business!

LEARN MORE. . .

Lynn offers a number of ways you can benefit from the practical application of intuition in your business and personal life.

Sign up for success.

Lynn's *Gut Trusters in Business* is a popular e-tips newsletter that provides powerful tools to help you build professional and personal success.

Get high-value information in seconds.

Lynn's on-the-spot intuitive insight offers immediate access to critical information that is difficult or impossible to get any other way. It's a major reason companies call on her for help with mergers, acquisitions, marketing, key hires, negotiations, and new business pitches.

Learn from Lynn in person.

Lynn is a professional speaker who consistently gets rave reviews for the depth of her content, her winning sense of humor, and her down-to-earth style. She offers keynote addresses, seminars, and half- or full-day training on the topic of intuition. Let her show you how to put intuition to profitable use in your business.

Contact: Lynn A. Robinson
Intuitive Consulting, Inc.
PO Box 81218
Wellesley Hills, MA 02481
(617) 964-0075
(800) 925-4002
e-mail: Lynn@LynnRobinson.com
Web site: *www.LynnRobinson.com*

3 5282 00646 5226